Family Law: A Very Short Introduction

VERY SHORT INTRODUCTIONS are for anyone wanting a stimulating and accessible way in to a new subject. They are written by experts, and have been translated into more than 40 different languages.

The Series began in 1995, and now covers a wide variety of topics in every discipline. The VSI library now contains over 350 volumes—a Very Short Introduction to everything from Psychology and Philosophy of Science to American History and Relativity—and continues to grow in every subject area.

Very Short Introductions available now:

ADVERTISING Winston Fletcher
AFRICAN HISTORY John Parker and Richard Rathbone
AFRICAN RELIGIONS Jacob K. Olupona
AGNOSTICISM Robin Le Poidevin
AMERICAN HISTORY Paul S. Boyer
AMERICAN IMMIGRATION David A. Gerber
AMERICAN LEGAL HISTORY G. Edward White
AMERICAN POLITICAL PARTIES AND ELECTIONS L. Sandy Maisel
AMERICAN POLITICS Richard M. Valelly
THE AMERICAN PRESIDENCY Charles O. Jones
ANAESTHESIA Aidan O'Donnell
ANARCHISM Colin Ward
ANCIENT EGYPT Ian Shaw
ANCIENT GREECE Paul Cartledge
THE ANCIENT NEAR EAST Amanda H. Podany
ANCIENT PHILOSOPHY Julia Annas
ANCIENT WARFARE Harry Sidebottom
ANGELS David Albert Jones
ANGLICANISM Mark Chapman
THE ANGLO-SAXON AGE John Blair
THE ANIMAL KINGDOM Peter Holland
ANIMAL RIGHTS David DeGrazia
THE ANTARCTIC Klaus Dodds
ANTISEMITISM Steven Beller
ANXIETY Daniel Freeman and Jason Freeman

THE APOCRYPHAL GOSPELS Paul Foster
ARCHAEOLOGY Paul Bahn
ARCHITECTURE Andrew Ballantyne
ARISTOCRACY William Doyle
ARISTOTLE Jonathan Barnes
ART HISTORY Dana Arnold
ART THEORY Cynthia Freeland
ASTROBIOLOGY David C. Catling
ATHEISM Julian Baggini
AUGUSTINE Henry Chadwick
AUSTRALIA Kenneth Morgan
AUTISM Uta Frith
THE AVANT GARDE David Cottington
THE AZTECS David Carrasco
BACTERIA Sebastian G. B. Amyes
BARTHES Jonathan Culler
THE BEATS David Sterritt
BEAUTY Roger Scruton
BESTSELLERS John Sutherland
THE BIBLE John Riches
BIBLICAL ARCHAEOLOGY Eric H. Cline
BIOGRAPHY Hermione Lee
THE BLUES Elijah Wald
THE BOOK OF MORMON Terryl Givens
BORDERS Alexander C. Diener and Joshua Hagen
THE BRAIN Michael O'Shea
THE BRITISH CONSTITUTION Martin Loughlin
THE BRITISH EMPIRE Ashley Jackson
BRITISH POLITICS Anthony Wright

BUDDHA Michael Carrithers
BUDDHISM Damien Keown
BUDDHIST ETHICS Damien Keown
CANCER Nicholas James
CAPITALISM James Fulcher
CATHOLICISM Gerald O'Collins
CAUSATION Stephen Mumford and
    Rani Lill Anjum
THE CELL Terence Allen and
    Graham Cowling
THE CELTS Barry Cunliffe
CHAOS Leonard Smith
CHILDREN'S LITERATURE
    Kimberley Reynolds
CHINESE LITERATURE
    Sabina Knight
CHOICE THEORY Michael Allingham
CHRISTIAN ART Beth Williamson
CHRISTIAN ETHICS D. Stephen Long
CHRISTIANITY Linda Woodhead
CITIZENSHIP Richard Bellamy
CIVIL ENGINEERING
    David Muir Wood
CLASSICAL MYTHOLOGY
    Helen Morales
CLASSICS Mary Beard and
    John Henderson
CLAUSEWITZ Michael Howard
CLIMATE Mark Maslin
THE COLD WAR Robert McMahon
COLONIAL AMERICA Alan Taylor
COLONIAL LATIN AMERICAN
    LITERATURE Rolena Adorno
COMEDY Matthew Bevis
COMMUNISM Leslie Holmes
THE COMPUTER Darrel Ince
THE CONQUISTADORS
    Matthew Restall and
    Felipe Fernández-Armesto
CONSCIENCE Paul Strohm
CONSCIOUSNESS Susan Blackmore
CONTEMPORARY ART
    Julian Stallabrass
CONTEMPORARY FICTION
    Robert Eaglestone
CONTINENTAL PHILOSOPHY
    Simon Critchley
COSMOLOGY Peter Coles
CRITICAL THEORY
    Stephen Eric Bronner

THE CRUSADES Christopher Tyerman
CRYPTOGRAPHY Fred Piper and
    Sean Murphy
THE CULTURAL REVOLUTION
    Richard Curt Kraus
DADA AND SURREALISM
    David Hopkins
DARWIN Jonathan Howard
THE DEAD SEA SCROLLS Timothy Lim
DEMOCRACY Bernard Crick
DERRIDA Simon Glendinning
DESCARTES Tom Sorell
DESERTS Nick Middleton
DESIGN John Heskett
DEVELOPMENTAL BIOLOGY
    Lewis Wolpert
THE DEVIL Darren Oldridge
DIASPORA Kevin Kenny
DICTIONARIES Lynda Mugglestone
DINOSAURS David Norman
DIPLOMACY Joseph M. Siracusa
DOCUMENTARY FILM
    Patricia Aufderheide
DREAMING J. Allan Hobson
DRUGS Leslie Iversen
DRUIDS Barry Cunliffe
EARLY MUSIC Thomas Forrest Kelly
THE EARTH Martin Redfern
ECONOMICS Partha Dasgupta
EDUCATION Gary Thomas
EGYPTIAN MYTH Geraldine Pinch
EIGHTEENTH-CENTURY BRITAIN
    Paul Langford
THE ELEMENTS Philip Ball
EMOTION Dylan Evans
EMPIRE Stephen Howe
ENGELS Terrell Carver
ENGINEERING David Blockley
ENGLISH LITERATURE Jonathan Bate
ENTREPRENEURSHIP
    Paul Westhead and Mike Wright
ENVIRONMENTAL ECONOMICS
    Stephen Smith
EPIDEMIOLOGY Rodolfo Saracci
ETHICS Simon Blackburn
ETHNOMUSICOLOGY Timothy Rice
THE EUROPEAN UNION
    John Pinder and Simon Usherwood
EVOLUTION Brian and
    Deborah Charlesworth

EXISTENTIALISM Thomas Flynn
FAMILY LAW Jonathan Herring
FASCISM Kevin Passmore
FASHION Rebecca Arnold
FEMINISM Margaret Walters
FILM Michael Wood
FILM MUSIC Kathryn Kalinak
THE FIRST WORLD WAR
    Michael Howard
FOLK MUSIC Mark Slobin
FOOD John Krebs
FORENSIC PSYCHOLOGY
    David Canter
FORENSIC SCIENCE Jim Fraser
FOSSILS Keith Thomson
FOUCAULT Gary Gutting
FRACTALS Kenneth Falconer
FREE SPEECH Nigel Warburton
FREE WILL Thomas Pink
FRENCH LITERATURE John D. Lyons
THE FRENCH REVOLUTION
    William Doyle
FREUD Anthony Storr
FUNDAMENTALISM Malise Ruthven
GALAXIES John Gribbin
GALILEO Stillman Drake
GAME THEORY Ken Binmore
GANDHI Bhikhu Parekh
GENIUS Andrew Robinson
GEOGRAPHY John Matthews and
    David Herbert
GEOPOLITICS Klaus Dodds
GERMAN LITERATURE
    Nicholas Boyle
GERMAN PHILOSOPHY
    Andrew Bowie
GLOBAL CATASTROPHES Bill McGuire
GLOBAL ECONOMIC HISTORY
    Robert C. Allen
GLOBAL WARMING Mark Maslin
GLOBALIZATION Manfred Steger
THE GOTHIC Nick Groom
GOVERNANCE Mark Bevir
THE GREAT DEPRESSION AND
    THE NEW DEAL Eric Rauchway
HABERMAS James Gordon Finlayson
HAPPINESS Daniel M. Haybron
HEGEL Peter Singer
HEIDEGGER Michael Inwood
HERODOTUS Jennifer T. Roberts

HIEROGLYPHS Penelope Wilson
HINDUISM Kim Knott
HISTORY John H. Arnold
THE HISTORY OF ASTRONOMY
    Michael Hoskin
THE HISTORY OF LIFE
    Michael Benton
THE HISTORY OF MATHEMATICS
    Jacqueline Stedall
THE HISTORY OF MEDICINE
    William Bynum
THE HISTORY OF TIME
    Leofranc Holford-Strevens
HIV/AIDS Alan Whiteside
HOBBES Richard Tuck
HUMAN EVOLUTION Bernard Wood
HUMAN RIGHTS Andrew Clapham
HUMANISM Stephen Law
HUME A. J. Ayer
HUMOUR Noël Carroll
IDEOLOGY Michael Freeden
INDIAN PHILOSOPHY Sue Hamilton
INFORMATION Luciano Floridi
INNOVATION Mark Dodgson and
    David Gann
INTELLIGENCE Ian J. Deary
INTERNATIONAL MIGRATION
    Khalid Koser
INTERNATIONAL RELATIONS
    Paul Wilkinson
INTERNATIONAL SECURITY
    Christopher S. Browning
ISLAM Malise Ruthven
ISLAMIC HISTORY Adam Silverstein
ITALIAN LITERATURE
    Peter Hainsworth and David Robey
JESUS Richard Bauckham
JOURNALISM Ian Hargreaves
JUDAISM Norman Solomon
JUNG Anthony Stevens
KABBALAH Joseph Dan
KAFKA Ritchie Robertson
KANT Roger Scruton
KEYNES Robert Skidelsky
KIERKEGAARD Patrick Gardiner
THE KORAN Michael Cook
LANDSCAPES AND
    GEOMORPHOLOGY
    Andrew Goudie and Heather Viles
LANGUAGES Stephen R. Anderson

LATE ANTIQUITY Gillian Clark
LAW Raymond Wacks
THE LAWS OF THERMODYNAMICS
    Peter Atkins
LEADERSHIP Keith Grint
LINCOLN Allen C. Guelzo
LINGUISTICS Peter Matthews
LITERARY THEORY Jonathan Culler
LOCKE John Dunn
LOGIC Graham Priest
MACHIAVELLI Quentin Skinner
MADNESS Andrew Scull
MAGIC Owen Davies
MAGNA CARTA Nicholas Vincent
MAGNETISM Stephen Blundell
MALTHUS Donald Winch
MANAGEMENT John Hendry
MAO Delia Davin
MARINE BIOLOGY Philip V. Mladenov
THE MARQUIS DE SADE John Phillips
MARTIN LUTHER Scott H. Hendrix
MARTYRDOM Jolyon Mitchell
MARX Peter Singer
MATHEMATICS Timothy Gowers
THE MEANING OF LIFE
    Terry Eagleton
MEDICAL ETHICS Tony Hope
MEDICAL LAW Charles Foster
MEDIEVAL BRITAIN
    John Gillingham and Ralph A. Griffiths
MEMORY Jonathan K. Foster
METAPHYSICS Stephen Mumford
MICHAEL FARADAY
    Frank A. J. L. James
MODERN ART David Cottington
MODERN CHINA Rana Mitter
MODERN FRANCE Vanessa R. Schwartz
MODERN IRELAND Senia Pašeta
MODERN JAPAN
    Christopher Goto-Jones
MODERN LATIN AMERICAN
    LITERATURE
    Roberto González Echevarría
MODERN WAR Richard English
MODERNISM Christopher Butler
MOLECULES Philip Ball
THE MONGOLS Morris Rossabi
MORMONISM
    Richard Lyman Bushman
MUHAMMAD Jonathan A. C. Brown

MULTICULTURALISM Ali Rattansi
MUSIC Nicholas Cook
MYTH Robert A. Segal
THE NAPOLEONIC WARS
    Mike Rapport
NATIONALISM Steven Grosby
NELSON MANDELA Elleke Boehmer
NEOLIBERALISM Manfred Steger and
    Ravi Roy
NETWORKS Guido Caldarelli and
    Michele Catanzaro
THE NEW TESTAMENT
    Luke Timothy Johnson
THE NEW TESTAMENT AS
    LITERATURE
    Kyle Keefer
NEWTON Robert Iliffe
NIETZSCHE Michael Tanner
NINETEENTH-CENTURY BRITAIN
    Christopher Harvie and
    H. C. G. Matthew
THE NORMAN CONQUEST
    George Garnett
NORTH AMERICAN INDIANS
    Theda Perdue and Michael D. Green
NORTHERN IRELAND
    Marc Mulholland
NOTHING Frank Close
NUCLEAR POWER Maxwell Irvine
NUCLEAR WEAPONS
    Joseph M. Siracusa
NUMBERS Peter M. Higgins
OBJECTIVITY Stephen Gaukroger
THE OLD TESTAMENT
    Michael D. Coogan
THE ORCHESTRA D. Kern Holoman
ORGANIZATIONS Mary Jo Hatch
PAGANISM Owen Davies
THE PALESTINIAN-ISRAELI CONFLICT
    Martin Bunton
PARTICLE PHYSICS Frank Close
PAUL E. P. Sanders
PENTECOSTALISM William K. Kay
THE PERIODIC TABLE Eric R. Scerri
PHILOSOPHY Edward Craig
PHILOSOPHY OF LAW
    Raymond Wacks
PHILOSOPHY OF SCIENCE
    Samir Okasha
PHOTOGRAPHY Steve Edwards

PLAGUE Paul Slack
PLANETS David A. Rothery
PLANTS Timothy Walker
PLATO Julia Annas
POLITICAL PHILOSOPHY
    David Miller
POLITICS Kenneth Minogue
POSTCOLONIALISM Robert Young
POSTMODERNISM Christopher Butler
POSTSTRUCTURALISM
    Catherine Belsey
PREHISTORY Chris Gosden
PRESOCRATIC PHILOSOPHY
    Catherine Osborne
PRIVACY Raymond Wacks
PROBABILITY John Haigh
PROGRESSIVISM Walter Nugent
PROTESTANTISM Mark A. Noll
PSYCHIATRY Tom Burns
PSYCHOLOGY Gillian Butler and
    Freda McManus
PURITANISM Francis J. Bremer
THE QUAKERS Pink Dandelion
QUANTUM THEORY
    John Polkinghorne
RACISM Ali Rattansi
RADIOACTIVITY Claudio Tuniz
RASTAFARI Ennis B. Edmonds
THE REAGAN REVOLUTION Gil Troy
REALITY Jan Westerhoff
THE REFORMATION Peter Marshall
RELATIVITY Russell Stannard
RELIGION IN AMERICA Timothy Beal
THE RENAISSANCE Jerry Brotton
RENAISSANCE ART
    Geraldine A. Johnson
RHETORIC Richard Toye
RISK Baruch Fischhoff and John Kadvany
RIVERS Nick Middleton
ROBOTICS Alan Winfield
ROMAN BRITAIN Peter Salway
THE ROMAN EMPIRE
    Christopher Kelly
THE ROMAN REPUBLIC
    David M. Gwynn
ROMANTICISM Michael Ferber
ROUSSEAU Robert Wokler
RUSSELL A. C. Grayling
RUSSIAN HISTORY Geoffrey Hosking
RUSSIAN LITERATURE Catriona Kelly

THE RUSSIAN REVOLUTION
    S. A. Smith
SCHIZOPHRENIA Chris Frith and
    Eve Johnstone
SCHOPENHAUER Christopher Janaway
SCIENCE AND RELIGION
    Thomas Dixon
SCIENCE FICTION David Seed
THE SCIENTIFIC REVOLUTION
    Lawrence M. Principe
SCOTLAND Rab Houston
SEXUALITY Véronique Mottier
SHAKESPEARE Germaine Greer
SIKHISM Eleanor Nesbitt
THE SILK ROAD James A. Millward
SLEEP Steven W. Lockley and
    Russell G. Foster
SOCIAL AND CULTURAL
    ANTHROPOLOGY
    John Monaghan and Peter Just
SOCIALISM Michael Newman
SOCIOLINGUISTICS John Edwards
SOCIOLOGY Steve Bruce
SOCRATES C. C. W. Taylor
THE SOVIET UNION Stephen Lovell
THE SPANISH CIVIL WAR
    Helen Graham
SPANISH LITERATURE Jo Labanyi
SPINOZA Roger Scruton
SPIRITUALITY Philip Sheldrake
STARS Andrew King
STATISTICS David J. Hand
STEM CELLS Jonathan Slack
STUART BRITAIN John Morrill
SUPERCONDUCTIVITY
    Stephen Blundell
SYMMETRY Ian Stewart
TERRORISM Charles Townshend
THEOLOGY David F. Ford
THOMAS AQUINAS Fergus Kerr
THOUGHT Tim Bayne
TIBETAN BUDDHISM
    Matthew T. Kapstein
TOCQUEVILLE Harvey C. Mansfield
TRAGEDY Adrian Poole
THE TROJAN WAR Eric H. Cline
TRUST Katherine Hawley
THE TUDORS John Guy
TWENTIETH-CENTURY BRITAIN
    Kenneth O. Morgan

THE UNITED NATIONS
    Jussi M. Hanhimäki
THE U.S. CONGRESS Donald A. Ritchie
THE U.S. SUPREME COURT
    Linda Greenhouse
UTOPIANISM Lyman Tower Sargent
THE VIKINGS Julian Richards
VIRUSES Dorothy H. Crawford

WITCHCRAFT Malcolm Gaskill
WITTGENSTEIN A. C. Grayling
WORK Stephen Fineman
WORLD MUSIC Philip Bohlman
THE WORLD TRADE ORGANIZATION
    Amrita Narlikar
WRITING AND SCRIPT
    Andrew Robinson

Available soon:

REVOLUTIONS Jack A. Goldstone
THE ICE AGE Jamie Woodward
TEETH Peter S. Ungar

ACCOUNTING Christopher Nobes
CLASSICAL LITERATURE
    William Allan

For more information visit our website
www.oup.com/vsi/

Jonathan Herring

FAMILY LAW

A Very Short Introduction

OXFORD
UNIVERSITY PRESS

OXFORD
UNIVERSITY PRESS

Great Clarendon Street, Oxford, ox2 6DP,
United Kingdom

Oxford University Press is a department of the University of Oxford.
It furthers the University's objective of excellence in research, scholarship,
and education by publishing worldwide. Oxford is a registered trade mark of
Oxford University Press in the UK and in certain other countries

Published in the United States of America by Oxford University Press
198 Madison Avenue, New York, NY 10016, United States of America

British Library Cataloguing in Publication Data
Data available

Library of Congress Control Number: 2013956955

ISBN 978-0-19-966852-6

Printed and bound by
CPI Group (UK) Ltd, Croydon, CR0 4YY

Contents

List of illustrations xiii

Introduction 1

1 Marriage, civil partnership, and cohabitation 2

2 Domestic violence 27

3 Divorce 42

4 Parents 52

5 Children's rights 67

6 Child abuse 79

7 Alimony and financial orders 92

8 Where next for family law? 109

Further reading 113

Index 117

List of illustrations

1 A typical 1970s family: father, mother, and two children **3**
© Dennis Hallinan/Getty Images

2 Same-sex marriage **16**
© Romain Beurrier/ Demotix/Demotix/Press Association Images

3 A poster encouraging women to report domestic violence **32**
Courtesy of the national domestic violence charity, Refuge

4 The moment of conception using IVF **54**
ZEPHYR/SCIENCE PHOTO LIBRARY

5 Do children have a right to refuse to eat broccoli? **69**
© Gallo Images/Alamy

6 An NSPCC poster informating people about child abuse **82**

7 Paul McCartney and Heather Mills **104**
© 2012 Photoshot/Getty Images

Introduction

Family life is changing at an extraordinary speed and family law is struggling to keep pace with what is happening. The standard building blocks of family law—marriage, parenthood, and childhood—are changing beyond recognition. We can no longer assume that marriage involves one man and one woman; that every child has one mother and one father; or that children need protection until they enter adulthood at age 18.

Family law is a fascinating area of study. It seeks to impose order on the chaos of people's intimate lives. While people will seek the advice of a lawyer before buying a house or executing a will, they, very sensibly, do not before having sex or moving in with a partner. The law is all too often left with a situation where there is no obviously correct answer which will leave everyone happy. Seeking the result which causes the least unhappiness is the more realistic solution.

This book does not seek to explain the law in any particular country in detail. Rather it explains the kinds of issues which family law must address and discusses the factors which influence its development. Examples are most commonly used from the US and UK, but the broader issues apply to any jurisdiction.

Chapter 1
Marriage, civil partnership, and cohabitation

Family life

What do you value most in your life? Surveys suggest that most people will say their family. But what exactly is a family?

A few decades ago there would have been widespread agreement over the answer to that question. A married couple with two children would be the archetype (see Figure 1). Nowadays any image of a typical family would raise controversy. It is interesting that at the same time the definition of family has broadened, the word family has come to have great significance. A group who thought of themselves as family but were told they would not be treated as a family would be likely to be severely offended. When the UK Conservative Government described a same-sex relationship as a 'pretended family relationship' in section 28 of the Local Government Act 1988, there was an outcry. Indeed it seems the wording was used specifically to denigrate gay relationships.

Our expected life stories have changed. In the past you might expect to be born to a mother and father, who were married; to grow up with your parents; and in due course you would be expected to marry and have children yourself. This life course is no longer predictable. Around half of children in the US and UK are born to unmarried couples. It is increasingly less likely

1. A typical 1970s family: father, mother, and two children

that a child will be raised consistently by their biological parents. There may be a series of adults who play parenting roles during a childhood because of increasing rates of relationship breakdown. Reproductive technology is such that a baby might be born to two women or two men or a larger group. Once an adult there are now a wide range of permutations of acceptable adult relationships you may adopt, including the increasingly popular option of living alone, and having a child on your own.

It is interesting too that family law has focused on marital and blood relationships and that friendships receive little or no legal

3

attention. You may spend more time with your friends than your family members, but to the law it is the family tie which carries the greater legal obligations. That may be because blood ties are easily provable, while the notion of friendship is somewhat opaque.

Marriage

For a long time marriage was at the heart of family law. Nowadays it plays a less significant role than it used to. It is generally agreed that parenthood is more significant as a source of legal rights and responsibility. Nevertheless a family lawyer could not advise a client properly without finding out whether they are married or not. Indeed, marriage has significance well beyond family law. In many countries your marital status can be important for the purposes of tax, inheritance law, social security provision, and so forth. In these ways being married amounts to the legally approved family form, which is given special privileges as a result.

Marriage has become a topic of huge social importance. Traditionally the concept of marriage was defined by religion and, in the Western world, Christianity in particular. However, the historical understanding of marriage has come under challenge from several sources. On the one hand there are those who argue that we need to rethink completely the traditional understanding of marriage and open it up to a far wider range of people. Most notably there are powerful calls to allow same-sex marriage, calls which traditionalists have fiercely rejected.

At the same time as some are fighting for the right for same-sex marriage, others are arguing that marriage should be treated as irrelevant. If a couple (or maybe more than two people) are in a stable relationship, whether they happen to have undertaken a formal ceremony a few years earlier should not be relevant to their legal status. We should, it is argued, focus on the quality of the relationship and not its official status.

What is marriage?

This question is at the heart of the debates over marriage. The difficulty is that there is no agreement on the answer. Martha Fineman, an American academic, has written of the diverse understandings of marriage:

> Marriage, to those involved in one, can mean a legal tie, a symbol of commitment, a privileged sexual affiliation, a relationship of hierarchy and subordination, a means of self-fulfilment, a social construct, a cultural phenomenon, a religious mandate, an economic relationship, the preferred unit for reproduction, a way to ensure against poverty and dependence on the state, a way out of the birth family, the realization of a romantic ideal, a natural or divine connection, a commitment to traditional notions of morality, a desired status that communicates one's sexual desirability to the world, or a purely contractual relationship in which each term is based on bargaining.

There is no single correct definition, of course, but the law needs to be clear that it is seeking to define the *legal* understanding of marriage, which is not the only perspective available. A Christian couple seeking to base their marriage on biblical principles may well see their marriage in very different terms from a couple who understand their marriage to be open and short-term, entered into for tax purposes. When Elizabeth I was queen of England, a common marriage vow of a wife was that she be 'bonny and buxom in bed and board'. As this indicates, expectations of the obligations of marriage have changed over time.

The ecclesiastical understanding of marriage which underpins the law in many Western countries is increasingly under challenge, especially given the diversity of views over matters of religion and even within religions. Most judges regard themselves as having a secular role, meaning they should not be seeking to enforce a particular religious view.

Indeed what the law is trying to do with the concept of marriage may well be very different from what religious doctrine is trying to do. The problem is that changing the legal definition of marriage is seen by some as an attack on a religious understanding. Of course, that need not be. There is nothing to stop a religion explaining how a religious concept of marriage is so much more meaningful than a legal one.

Despite the impression given in TV dramas, only a minority of the adult population are married in most Western countries. In the UK 44 per cent of households including an adult under the age of 65 include a married couple. Marriage rates are declining. In the US the number of people per thousand marrying in a given year has fallen from 8.2 in 2000 to 6.8 in 2011. For England the rates are higher, but show a similar decrease from 10.3 to 8.7. It is not just the number of marriages which is declining. Its nature is changing. People are marrying later; cohabitation prior to marriage is normal; and the likelihood that marriage will end in divorce has greatly increased.

Legal definitions of marriage

A commonly cited definition of marriage in US and UK law is that from the 1866 case of *Hyde v Hyde and Woodhouse*: 'the voluntary union for life of one man and one woman to the exclusion of all others'. However, this cannot be understood as a legal definition. It is now quite possible to have a legally valid marriage which is entered into involuntarily, is characterized by sexual unfaithfulness, and is ended by divorce. At best the statement can be seen as an ideal of marriage the law wishes to promote. By way of contrast, an English judge, Thorpe LJ, has provided a more recent definition of marriage:

> a contract for which the parties elect but which is regulated by the state, both in its formation and in its termination by divorce because it affects status upon which depend a variety of entitlements, benefits and obligations.

Notably this has no requirement that the parties are the opposite sex; that the marriage is for life; or monogamous. Indeed it seems only the 'voluntariness' element of the *Hyde* definition remains in his formulation. Not all judges are open to such a broad understanding of marriage. Lord Millet has stated:

> Marriage is the lawful union of a man and a woman. It is a legal relationship between persons of the opposite sex. A man's spouse must be a woman; a woman's spouse must be a man. This is of the very essence of the relationship, which need not be loving, sexual, stable, faithful, long-lasting, or contented.

Much of the discussion among the American judiciary has emphasized marriage as a constitutional right, protected under the fourteenth amendment of the US constitution. In the famous case of *Loving v Virginia* (1967) the US Supreme Court struck down as unconstitutional a statute which did not allow a man and woman to marry because of their race. Chief Justice Warren held:

> The freedom to marry has long been recognized as one of the vital personal rights essential to the orderly pursuit of happiness by free men.

As this discussion shows, it is somewhat difficult to produce a definitive definition of marriage. The reason is this. The law contains detailed regulations about who can marry whom; what ceremony needs to be undertaken in order to create a marriage; and rules on the financial consequences at the end of a marriage. However, the behaviour of married couples is unregulated, save, for example, the law on domestic abuse. Perhaps this is a recognition that people will arrange their marriages in many different ways and it is not possible to identify a single mode of marriage that the law should enforce. However, this has the surprising result that the law will permit marriages entered into for 'improper' purposes such as immigration or tax purposes. It is not for the law to decide whether the marriage is entered into for a good reason.

Marriage as a status or a contract

One major debate is over the extent to which marriage should be regarded as a contract. Different jurisdictions have taken disparate views on this. On the other hand, the 'status' camp regards marriage as a legal relationship from which a set of consequences flow automatically, regardless of the intention of the parties. It is a little like joining a club which has a set of rules. You can join the club and agree to abide by the rules, but you cannot join and choose which rules you wish to follow. The contract view of marriage believes that the legal consequences of marriage should be determined by the parties themselves by entering a contract. It is wrong, supporters of this approach claim, to have a fixed model of marriage and people must 'like it or lump it'. Rather each party should be free to determine what version of the model works well for them.

There are, of course, some middle routes between status and contract views of marriage. One would be for the state to offer a range of alternative marriage models which individuals can choose from. In some states in the US the option of a 'covenant marriage' is offered as an alternative to the standard model. Covenant marriage has a stricter divorce law and is designed to appeal to those seeking a more traditional version of marriage. Shia Islamic Law offers fixed term marriages.

Another middle route would be for the law to have a standard model of marriage, but allow the parties to alter the standard form through a pre-marriage contract. We shall explore these in Chapter 7, but for the moment we should note that where they are given effect to they enable couples to depart from the standard model promoted by the law.

Notice, that if the more contractarian approach is taken it becomes difficult to promote marriage as an institution. It loosens any particular meaning, and that meaning varies for each marriage. But, some will feel, that is as it should be. In societies with a broad range of cultural, religious, and moral views on marriage the law should not seek to maintain one particular version, but give the space for each couple to shape their own.

Proving marriage

Most countries have a system of registration of marriage, whereby on marriage a formal record is made of the ceremony. This means that if in the future it is unclear whether a couple are married or not a simple check on the register can find out the truth. However, it is not always that straightforward. Two situations can create difficulties. First, there are cases where the couple believe they have gone through a ceremony of marriage, often a religious one, but it is one which (unknown to them) is in fact an invalid ceremony in terms of the legal requirement. Second, there are situations where the couple have married overseas but it is impossible to obtain evidence whether or not the couple are indeed married.

The first kind of case is problematic. On the one hand the law wishes to ensure that the legal formalities accompanying marriage are complied with. If the law becomes lax in relation to enforcement of these then they may become routinely ignored. On the other hand, where a couple believe they have married and are just ignorant of the legal requirements it seems harsh simply to treat them as unmarried. A common approach, taken by the American and English courts, is to allow the marriage to stand where the couple were unaware of the procedural defect and were genuinely attempting to conduct a legal marriage.

In the second kind of case, common law jurisdictions have developed a presumption that a couple who have cohabited for a considerable period of time, regard themselves as married and are regarded in the wider community as married, are indeed married. That presumption is rebuttable. This assists couples who struggle to prove they were married overseas as the burden lies on those who seek to deny their marriage.

Void, voidable, and non-marriages

An apparent marriage which is invalid may be regarded by the courts as a void marriage or a voidable marriage. This arcane differentiation has an important theoretical distinction. A *void* marriage is not, never has been, and never will be a marriage. There is no need for a court order to declare the marriage void because it never existed in the first place, although a party might seek a court order by way of confirmation. Anyone with a legitimate interest can seek a court declaration that a marriage is void. A *voidable* marriage on the other hand is a perfectly valid marriage until a party seeks to set it aside. Indeed, if no application is made it will remain as much a valid marriage as any other. Further, only the parties themselves can apply for the marriage to be annulled. These differences reflect a deeper significance of the concepts. The grounds on which a marriage is void in the law are those for which there is a public policy objection to the marriage. Hence it simply is not allowed to exist and any interested party can seek a court declaration. The grounds on which a marriage is voidable are not those which relate to a public policy objection to the marriage, but are matters which the law accepts a party might regard as so fundamental to a marriage that they indicate the marriage is fundamentally flawed at its inception and so it should be dissolved. It should be noted here that nullity is different from divorce. Divorce accepts that a valid marriage has come to an end. Nullity is claiming that there never was a proper marriage.

Void marriages

American and English law have similar grounds for a marriage being void, although they differ somewhat in their details:

- That the parties are within 'a prohibited degree of relationship' (e.g. they are siblings)

- Either party is under age (this varies between 16 and 18 between states)

- The parties have knowingly and wilfully married in breach of the formality requirements (e.g. that the ceremony did not take place before an appropriate official)
- That the parties are not respectively male and female
- That the parties are already married to someone else

The age and formality requirements are relatively uncontroversial. The prohibited degrees of relationship reflect a worldwide and long-lasting assumption that marriage between closely related people is inappropriate. The exact list of prohibited relationships varies slightly from jurisdiction to jurisdiction, for example cousins are permitted to marry in the UK, but not in many states of the US. US states vary in the extent to which adopted relatives can marry. But all jurisdictions prohibit marriage between parents and children; grandparents and grandchildren; and siblings. These restrictions are justified in part by a concern that the offspring of closely related couples might be affected by genetic disorders. However, it might be argued that the strength of this argument is lessened given the availability of genetic screening. Some jurisdictions extend beyond these blood relations, to relations based on marriage, prohibiting, for example, someone marrying their father-in-law or step-child. Others rely on the deep intuition (or 'yuck factor') against incest that is so widespread that it must reflect a truth beyond our ken. Perhaps the most convincing explanation is that children should be brought up without the possibility of approved sexual relations later in life with members of their family.

Most Western countries do not permit polygamy (the having of more than one spouse). According to the American Model Penal Code (section 230.1) bigamy is a misdemeanour, but having more than one spouse at the same time is a felony if it is done 'in purported exercise of a plural marriage'. Again it is not straightforward to explain what is objectionable to polygamy.

Within mainstream Christianity marriage and common law jurisdictions marriage has been understood as being restricted to two people. However, other countries and religions, notably branches of Islam, have taken a different view and have been open to polygamous marriage. An argument might be made that polygamous marriage can create tensions between the spouses or the children of the spouses and that is undesirable, although it is debatable whether there is much evidence to support that thesis. More persuasive may be an argument that polygamous marriages are commonly ones reflecting social attitudes which are negative about women. Women should be an equal partner in a marriage, and not in a subservient, powerless role.

It is the requirement that the parties be male and female which creates the most controversies. This raises two primary issues.

First, the definition of male and female needs to be considered. As the law requires the parties to marriage to be male and female it must go on to define what exactly is meant by those terms. That is far from straightforward! The English and American courts have taken different approaches (see Box 1).

Box 1 *Corbett v Corbett* (1971)

Ashley Corbett was registered as a boy at birth. In adulthood she underwent gender reassignment surgery and lived as a woman. She married a man. The marriage was not a success and the husband sought to have the marriage annulled. Ormrod J, who had the benefit of being a qualified doctor as well as a judge, determined that sex was fixed at birth and was based on three biological factors: genital, chromosomal, and gonadal. For Ashley at her birth these were all male. The fact that she was currently living as a woman was beside the point, her sex of male was fixed at birth.

Box 2 *M.T. v J.T.* (1976)

The plaintiff was born a man, but now lived as a woman. The court took account of both her physical and psychological attributes. Following her gender reassignment surgery her physical and psychological attributes had been unified as female. The court took the view it was giving legal effect to 'fait accompli'. It added that recognizing the plaintiff as male will 'promote the individual's quest for inner peace and personal happiness, while in no way disserving any societal interest, principle of public order or precept of morality'.

Notably the *Corbett* approach was rejected by the American courts (see Box 2).

English law has developed to restrict the *Corbett* analysis. After several unsuccessful challenges the European Court of Human Rights eventually determined that the failure of the law to recognize a person as having the sex they lived in amounted to a breach of human rights. English law responded to the decision with the Gender Recognition Act 2004, which allows a person who has received treatment for gender dysphoria to receive a certificate acknowledging that they are now to be regarded as being of their 'acquired gender'. Most US states have similar legislation.

The current law in most countries does not deal properly with intersex people. That is, those who at birth are ambiguous in relation to their biological sex. Some intersex people will regard themselves as male or female and the law is likely to respect that choice. However, there is no option for people to declare they are neither male nor female. Indeed some considering the position of intersex people have argued that it would be more accurate if the law were to recognize that the biological reality is that there are not two clearly differentiated boxes, male and female, but rather a scale of sexual identity from male to female. The law is a long way from recognizing that.

A second issue raised by the requirement that parties to a marriage be male and female is same-sex marriage. That will be addressed shortly.

Voidable marriages

Remember that a voidable marriage is one which is valid, but which either party is entitled to have set aside and when such an order is made, it is as if there was no marriage. There are two main areas: consummation and failure to consent.

The English law on voidable marriages is dominated by non-consummation, due to either the incapacity of either party or the wilful refusal of the party who is not applying to have the marriage annulled. Consummation takes place if there is an act of sexual intercourse after the marriage. The requirement is difficult to explain except as a vestige of the ecclesiastical doctrine that an act of consummation was required to reflect and complete the spiritual union that takes place on marriage. American law does not have any provision dealing with consummation. It is rarely used in English law today.

The other main issue in voidable marriages is a failure to consent, as a result of pressure or deceptions; and these are elements of both American and English law. There are two major issues here. The first is forced marriages. These are marriages where improper pressure is imposed by parents or other relatives. It is important to distinguish forced marriages from the practice of arranged marriages, where parents find a suitable partner for their adult child. As long as the adult child genuinely agrees to such a marriage there is no problem. It is where violence, threats of violence, strong emotional pressure, or economic threats are used to compel an adult child to marry that the concerns are raised. The courts recognize there is a difficult balancing act to be carried out between allowing parents to encourage children to follow their wishes and where the pressure used becomes such that there is no genuine consent.

The second issue is where the party has tricked the other party into marriage. There is an interesting difference here between American law and English law. Under American law a deception as to an 'essential matter' can render a marriage voidable. This has been interpreted fairly widely. In *Bilowit v Dolitsky* (1973) the husband deceived his wife about his religious beliefs (something very important to the wife) and that was sufficient to have the marriage annulled. However, the courts are generally reluctant to allow deceptions about a person's temperament or character to be included. English law has taken a more restrictive approach to the issue of mistakes and will only annul a marriage where there has been a mistake of identity. For example, where a woman has married a man, believing she was marrying his twin brother.

Mental disorder and marriage

This is a particularly tricky issue. What degree of mental capacity is required so that a person can marry? The problem is that if we are too strict about what counts as capacity for marriage then people with mild learning difficulties will be unable to marry. While if we are too lax about the capacity required to marry then a person may be married without being aware of the nature of what they are entering into. The courts tend to take the view that as long as the couple understand the key elements of marriage, that they are to live together and be faithful, that is sufficient. They do not need to understand all the legal niceties. The courts have acknowledged the danger here of merging the questions of whether a person has the capacity to enter a marriage and whether a marriage is wise. That is a particularly difficult line to draw where the feeling is that a vulnerable person has been exploited.

Same-sex marriage or civil partnership

In many countries same-sex behaviour (see Figure 2) between men has historically been unlawful. It is possible to identify a journey which many countries have already taken in response to same-sex couples. First, the law removes criminal offences outlawing same-sex activity. Second, the law grants same-sex couples an increasing set of rights. Third, a status equivalent to marriage, but different from it, is granted to same-sex couples. Finally, same-sex couples are allowed to marry.

At the time of writing Argentina, Belgium, Canada, Denmark, France, Iceland, the Netherlands, Norway, Portugal, Spain, South Africa, and Sweden all allow same-sex marriage. Other countries, including England, are in the process of introducing it. Some states in the US permit it.

Some countries have preferred to allow same-sex couples to enter a relationship which is similar to marriage. For example, in

2. **Same-sex marriage**

England the Civil Partnership Act 2004 allows same-sex couples to have a civil partnership and this is akin to marriage in all but name. Apart from a few technical differences the legal rights in marriage and civil partnership are identical. To some that means there is no need to move to same-sex marriage because civil partnership gives same-sex couples all the legal rights they need. But to others, if the institutions are identical why use a different name? Doing so implies a second-class citizenship. In jurisdictions such as these the fact that the debate continues shows the significance the name 'marriage' can still carry.

So what are the key features in the debates over same-sex marriage? The most vocal opposition comes from religious groups. To them the nature of marriage is fixed in tradition and has a special religious meaning. They feel the law should respect and uphold the traditional religious meaning, recognizing that, historically, marriage emanates from religion, rather than law. Many of those from this perspective have much less of a problem with the idea of civil partnerships because this status does not challenge the religious conception. Others will question whether the law should seek to uphold the religious concept. They feel that just because the law and religion use the word 'marriage' does not mean the law has to adopt the religious understanding of marriage. In fact, even among religious groups many support same-sex marriage. This highlights that it is not simply a matter of the law preferring a secular view of marriage over a religious one. Even if the law is to uphold a religious view, which religious view should it uphold?

The argument against same-sex marriage might also be put in terms of understanding the offence caused to those with strong religious views on marriage. If civil partnership can give same-sex couples all the benefits of marriage, without causing offence, is that not a good compromise? However, even accepting that permitting same-sex marriage would cause offence to some religious believers, is that offence greater than the offence to same-sex couples who wish to marry but cannot? In *Home Affairs v Fourie* (2005), a South African case, Justice Albie Sachs argued:

> The exclusion of same sex couples from the benefits and responsibilities of marriage, accordingly, is not a small and tangential inconvenience resulting from a few surviving relics of societal prejudice destined to evaporate like the morning dew. It represents a harsh if oblique statement by the law that same sex couples are outsiders, and that their need for affirmation and protection of their intimate relations as human beings is somehow less than that of heterosexual couples. It reinforces the wounding notion that they are to be treated as biological oddities, as failed or lapsed human beings who do not fit into normal society, and, as such, do not qualify for the full moral concern and respect that our Constitution seeks to secure for everyone. It signifies that their capacity for love, commitment and accepting responsibility is by definition less worthy of regard than that of heterosexual couples.

This quote captures well many of the arguments in favour of same-sex marriage. Same-sex relationships typically reflect the values that we seek to promote in marriage of love, mutual care, and support. They deserve equal respect with opposite-sex relationships.

Other arguments against same-sex marriage are that the production and care of children is a central aspect of marriage. However, this argument is less convincing given that many married couples don't have children and many same-sex couples do produce children (with assisted reproduction and/or surrogacy) and raise them well. This then raises the question, if marriage is not about producing children what is it about? Patrick Parkinson, a leading Australian academic opposing same-sex marriage, has written:

> A consequence of extending marriage to same-sex relationships is that there will be almost nothing left of the legal definition of marriage as a union of a man and a woman for life to the exclusion

of all others. Robbed of its distinctiveness, and detached from its cultural and religious roots, marriage as an institution is unlikely to retain its cultural importance and vitality. We simply won't know what marriage is any more.

This does raise the central issue: what is marriage about? This arose in a case before the European Court of Human Rights: *Burden v UK* (2008) where two unmarried sisters had lived together for many years. They were concerned that if either of them died the other would be liable to pay inheritance tax. They complained to the European Court of Human Rights that they were denied the exemption from inheritance tax that was available to married couples and civil partners. The Grand Chamber of the ECtHR rejected their complaint stating that a relationship between siblings is 'qualitatively of a different nature to that between married couples and [civil partners]...The very essence of the connection between siblings is consanguity, whereas one of the defining characteristics of a marriage or Civil Partnership Act union is that it is forbidden to close family members.' The court went on to explain that what is special about a civil partnership is the existence of a public undertaking and the rights and obligations that go with that. This public undertaking and acceptance of responsibilities makes civil partnership (and marriage) different from cohabitation. This reasoning will not convince everyone.

I have made a more radical suggestion that we need a 'sexless family law': one where the central focus of the law is not on sexual relationship, but rather on the care given within a relationship. 'Caring relationships' rather than 'sexual relationships' should be the standard. This would see those relationships which require especial protection and promotion in the law as not being sexual ones, but ones based on the care of a dependant or the mutual care of each other. It is these relationships which are essential to society's well-being and which need the protection and promotion of the law. In short if the government announced a 'no sex month' it might be somewhat frustrating, but we would survive. If it announced a 'no care month' society would collapse and serious harm would follow.

Unregulated relationships

One of the most tricky issues in family law is how to deal with couples who have not decided to formalize their relationships by, for example, getting married or entering a civil partnership. A particular difficulty is that such couples cover a wide range of relationships. While couples who have married or entered a civil partnership can be taken to intend a relationship which has legal consequences and has a degree of permanence, the same cannot be said of a cohabiting couple. It may be they are a couple who regard their relationship as lifelong and intend legal protections, but have never got around to it. On the other hand, they may be intending their relationship to be a casual, informal one. Indeed it may be they are cohabiting but simply for convenience and their relationship is not particularly close. Given this diversity, it is unlikely a single approach can govern all cohabiting relationships. Barlow, Burgoyne, and Smithson, British researchers, have suggested there are essentially four categories of cohabitants:

- the Ideologues: those in long-term relationships, but with an ideological objection to marriage;
- the Romantics: those who expect to get married eventually and see cohabitation as a step towards marriage, which they see as a serious commitment;
- the Pragmatists: those who decide whether or not to get married on legal or financial grounds;
- the Uneven Couples: where one partner wanted to marry and the other did not.

More and more couples are choosing to live together without marrying and around half of all children are born to unmarried couples in both the US and England. This makes the legal response to these informal relationships an important practical issue.

Before exploring this further it is worth looking at the differences between the legal regulation of a married couple and an unmarried couple. Surprisingly these are few. The most notable ones occur when the relationship comes to an end. We will take this further in Chapter 7 but for a married couple the court has considerable power to redistribute the couple's property, while for an unmarried couple each party can keep their own property.

Usually the courts give unmarried couples no special regulation and when they separate they must rely on the normal law. However, sometimes the courts have been creative in using the standard legal tools. Box 3 details one of the most famous American cases on the issue.

Should there be any difference between married and cohabiting couples? To some commentators, choice is the key factor.

Box 3 *Marvin v Marvin* (1964)

The actor Lee Marvin started living with his partner Michelle. They lived together for six years, but never married. Michelle could not make a financial claim against him based on their relationship because they were unmarried. However, she claimed that the couple had an oral agreement to share their property. Alternatively she argued that a constructive trust could be imposed on the property acquired during their lives together. The Supreme Court of California rejected the argument that to enforce any agreement between them would be contrary to public policy. The case was remanded to be reheard to determine whether or not such an agreement existed. In subsequent litigation Michelle failed to establish any claim.

The state has provided the possibility of marriage or other ways of regulating a relationship. If a couple choose not to enter that, it would be wrong to impose upon them legal consequences which they do not seek and may even be actively trying to avoid. We should treat them as any two other individuals. That means they can use the normal law of crime, contract, or tort, but they have no special remedies flowing from their relationship.

At first sight this is an appealing argument. It respects the individual choice of the couple. To say to a couple who have deliberately decided to avoid the consequences of marriage, 'we are going to treat you as if you are married' seems to show a lack of respect for their autonomy. However, the issue is not that straightforward. First, one difficulty is that the public may misunderstand the current legal position. In England, for example, there is a widespread assumption that couples who have lived together for two years are treated as being married. That is a false belief, but it is prevalent, supported to some extent by the media. So couples who are cohabiting have not necessarily rejected legal regulation—they might assume it is applicable in their relationship. Second, studies of unmarried couples commonly find that many have not chosen to avoid legal regulation, but have never got around to it. Third, there may be some couples who disagree whether or not to marry. We cannot take it that they have both agreed not to have legal consequences attached to their relationship. Fourth, and most importantly, it may be argued that justice calls out for some consequences to flow from a relationship and couples should not be able to choose to opt out of justice. For example, we might say that if a man moves in with a woman and they have four children together, he should not be able to choose to walk away with no responsibilities to them.

Some people argue that the state should seek to encourage marriage because it creates more stable relationships, and that treating married and unmarried couples in the same way undermines marriage. There is much debate over the statistics.

In the UK, the Conservative Party's Centre for Social Justice claims that those children not in two-parent families are:

- 75 per cent more likely to fail at school
- 70 per cent more likely to be a drug addict
- 50 per cent more likely to have an alcohol problem
- 40 per cent more likely to have serious debt problems
- 35 per cent more likely to experience unemployment/welfare dependency

They go on to argue that because marriage secures relationships, parents should be encouraged to marry.

In the US, the National Marriage Project, involving a range of pressure groups, found twenty-six disadvantages to cohabitation, as compared to being married, including:

- Higher level of abuse
- Increased levels of anxiety
- Greater difficulty in resolving conflict
- Less satisfactory sex lives
- Enhanced risk of premature death

However, in response, some commentators point out that these statistics are unsurprising given that marriage is more popular among better-off couples. These statistics may reflect the relative poverty of unmarried parents, rather than their lack of adequate parenting. Indeed it is hard to believe when thinking about a person with alcohol problems, for example, that their problems would not be there if only their parents had spent a short time in a registry office before their conception.

There are similar debates over whether unmarried couples are more likely to break up than married couples. After an extensive review of the literature researchers Alissa Goodman and Ellen Greaves conclude:

Our findings suggest that while it is true that cohabiting parents are more likely to split up than married ones, there is very little evidence to suggest that this is due to a causal effect of marriage. Instead, it seems simply that different sorts of people choose to get married and have children, rather than to have children as a cohabiting couple, and that those relationships with the best prospects of lasting are the ones that are most likely to lead to marriage.

These points do not necessarily suggest that marriage is of no benefit. Marriage seems to provide a social structure and support for a relationship, and is a socially acknowledged way of expressing and undertaking commitment. However, they do suggest that marriage should not be regarded as the only way of securing a relationship.

To some people the legal consequences of marriage flow not so much from the technical form of the relationship, but rather what has occurred in it. Should it matter that much to their relations whether a couple happened to have spent a few minutes in a ceremony, maybe years ago? Take a domestic violence case. If a man has beaten up his partner and she is seeking legal orders protecting her, whether or not they are married is irrelevant to the appropriate legal response. Even in relation to financial orders, if a couple have had children together and shared their lives, is whether twenty years ago they went through a marriage ceremony that relevant?

One option is to presume marriage after a certain period of cohabitation. We might say that if a couple have lived together for, say, two or five years, they will be treated as married. Many who support such a proposal would add that there could be an opt-out arrangement if a couple wished to avoid that consequence. But to some this kind of presumed marriage undermines the concept of marriage. It should be a status you choose to take on, rather than an obligation imposed upon you by default.

A common solution in most countries is that some consequences of marriage apply to an unmarried couple, but not all. So, we might say that in relation to domestic violence there will be no difference in the legal response whether the couple are married or not. However, in relation to inheritance, there will be a difference. Even where there is a difference it need not follow that no legal results will flow from the relationship, for example in relation to financial issues and cohabitation the law might say that there will be some redistribution of property but the financial consequences flowing from a cohabiting relationship will not be the same as marriage.

It is certainly true that the differences between married and unmarried couples are being reduced. In many countries there used to be tax advantages to being married, now these are only very limited in most countries. Indeed for some couples in tax terms they would be better off being unmarried. Also, there used to be significant differences between parents who were married or unmarried. Children born to unmarried couples were seen as 'illegitimate' and their parents had only very limited rights over them. Nowadays children will be treated no differently whether their parents are married or not.

Is marriage past its sell-by date?

Perhaps the time has come to question whether marriage is useful as a legal institution. There is no doubt it will continue as a religious and social institution, but should the law take account of it? There is no doubt that marriage has a miserable history. It has been used to perpetuate a disadvantage to women; to justify domestic violence; and to devalue care work. However, this is true of a range of social institutions. The real question is whether a modern understanding of marriage based on a partnership of equals, sharing the burdens of homemaking, child-caring, and wealth creation, has a public benefit.

I would argue it has. We need an institution which promotes intimate relationships of care; ensures that there is protection if abuse occurs within those relationships; and regulates the consequences of the breakdown of those relationships. Marriage has the capability of providing that. However, if marriage is to perform this new role it will need to be rethought and better understood. And if the religious and cultural meaning attached to marriage prevents a modern undertaking, then leaving marriage as a religious ceremony and instituting a new form of legal partnership for all, regardless of their religion or gender, might be the fairest way forward. The law is meant to enable and protect, and we are at our most vulnerable in relationships. That is why this is such an important and emotive issue.

Chapter 2
Domestic violence

Christopher Lasch, a sociologist, described the home as 'a haven in a heartless world': a place of security, comfort, and peace, away from the travails of reality. All too often it is a place of violence and terror. However, it is only relatively recently that the issues of domestic abuse and child abuse have revealed publicly the popular image as false. In fact, as Antony Giddens, a prominent sociologist, claims:

> The home is in fact the most dangerous place in modern society. In statistical terms, a person of any age or of either sex is far more likely to be subject to physical attack in the home than on the street at night.

The law in all jurisdictions has been reluctant to interfere in cases of domestic abuse. Only in the last few decades has the law begun to accept that domestic abuse is a serious social problem that requires an effective legal response. For too long violence in the home was dismissed as part of the 'rough and tumble of family life' or a private matter of no relevance to the state. Nowadays there is general acceptance that domestic violence is an issue of major social importance: it blights the lives of victims; it contributes to disadvantage against women; and it carries enormous costs to the community. Despite the growing acknowledgement that the issue is important there is fierce debate over the correct response of the law to it.

What is domestic violence?

There is no agreement over how to define domestic violence. At one time it was common to talk about 'battered wives' but, of course, not all the victims are wives, nor women; and not all domestic violence involves battery. The US Department of Justice uses this definition

> We define domestic violence as a pattern of abusive behavior in any relationship that is used by one partner to gain or maintain power and control over another intimate partner. Domestic violence can be physical, sexual, emotional, economic, or psychological actions or threats of actions that influence another person. This includes any behaviors that intimidate, manipulate, humiliate, isolate, frighten, terrorize, coerce, threaten, blame, hurt, injure, or wound someone.

There are several things that are notable about this definition. First, it extends domestic violence well beyond cases of straightforward violence and includes matters such as emotional and financial abuse, which would not constitute assaults in their traditional sense. Second, it appreciates that domestic abuse is best understood in the context of a relationship, describing it as a pattern of behaviour of coercive control. This is important because looking at a single incident of abuse will not capture the true nature of behaviour which can only be understood when looking at the overall relationship. Third, domestic violence is not restricted to married or cohabiting couples but includes all who live in an intimate relationship.

American academic Michelle Madden Dempsey has helpfully listed three factors which are linked with domestic violence:

- Illegitimate violence
- Domesticity
- Structural inequality.

She suggests where all three are present there is domestic violence in the strong sense, whereas domestic violence in the weak sense arises where there is domesticity and structural inequality.

Illegitimate violence

Illegitimate violence refers to those acts of violence which are not justified. Acts of violence which are justified, such as acts in self-defence, are not treated as domestic violence. This is relatively uncontroversial. There is much dispute, however, over whether the term domestic violence should be restricted to acts of physical aggression. As we have seen the new definition of domestic violence offered by the UK Government focuses on coercive control, which need not involve violence. Not everyone is happy with this move. Some believe that we should limit the definition of domestic abuse to physical assaults because that is the most serious kind of abuse. It must be admitted that normally in the law physical attacks are treated more seriously than emotional abuse. Madden Dempsey takes a middle route, suggesting that cases where there is no physical violence are domestic violence, but only in the weak sense.

So what reasons might there be for extending domestic violence beyond the notion of violence?

The answer lies in the concept of coercive control that we have already mentioned. Victims of domestic violence commonly report that the nature of the wrong they suffered cannot be described in terms simply of the incidents of physical assault, but the role these assaults played in the broader context of a relationship within which their freedom and self-worth were destroyed. The violence was simply a tool used to effect control. Indeed once control is achieved little actual violence may be required to continue the domination. So, an approach which focuses on the control of the victim better captures the wrong of domestic abuse.

Domesticity

Domesticity captures the argument that the particular wrong of domestic violence is most apparent when the couple is living together or in a close emotional relationship. This is the distinction between an assault in the street and a domestic assault. At one time campaigners for domestic violence worked hard to argue that an assault in the home should be taken as seriously as an attack in the street. However, now a good argument can be made for saying that domestic assaults are worse than street assaults. First, domestic assaults commonly are part of an abusive relationship which severely limits the freedom of the victim, to a greater extent than a stranger assault. Second, domestic violence involves a major breach of trust, unlike a stranger attack. Third, domestic violence means using what should be a source of strength and personal identity for the victim (a close relationship) against herself.

Structural inequality

Madden Dempsey sees this third element as central because it captures the notion of inequality within the relationship. This helps distinguish between an act of violence in what is otherwise an equal relationship between the parties and an act of violence which is part of an ongoing relationship of oppression. This is not to downplay the severity of the isolated act of violence, but to acknowledge than an extra dimension is added when it is part of the ongoing relationship of inequality.

However, there is more to the idea of structural inequality than simply the issue of inequality within the relationship itself. Domestic violence reflects and reinforces social forces that work against the interests of women. A domestic abuser typically seeks to restrict the woman to perform the role expected of the 'traditional wife': to cook, clean, service, and be obedient. Women are expected to be quiet and not step beyond their role. A common feature of domestic abuse relationships is that the man seeks to prevent the woman working outside the home. His efforts combine with the broader difficulties that society places in the way of women, especially those with children, from finding employment.

What is helpful about Madden Dempsey's analysis is, first, that it shows that we need not take a black and white approach and say that an incident either is or is not domestic violence. Second, it helps identify the precise wrong that has taken place and so distinguish between a case of 'intimate terrorism' (to use a phrase of academic Michael Johnson) and 'violent resistance' where an argument between partners gets ugly in a relationship which is generally equal.

Gender and domestic violence

Most domestic violence takes place against women. However, it would be wrong to think that men are not subjected to violence by their partners. Interestingly some studies find that there is not a large difference between the number of cases where men use physical force against women and where women use it against men. But, and it's a big but, the context of women's violence against men is very different. It tends to be cases of self-defence and it normally causes far less injury to the victim than man on woman violence. Only very rarely is woman on man violence part of a relationship marked by coercive control of the man by the woman. That said, there are quite a number of cases where men are abused by women. These men are normally very reluctant to come forward to seek help due to the stigma that attaches to it.

Statistics on domestic violence

Domestic violence is the largest cause of morbidity worldwide in women aged 19–44, exceeding war, cancer, or road traffic accidents (see Figure 3). According to the WHO, although domestic abuse occurs in all societies, its rate varies. It found

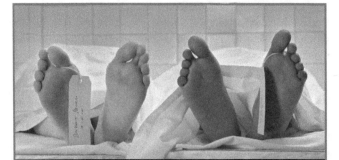

Every week, another two women escape domestic violence.

According to the Home Office, two women in England and Wales are killed by their partner or ex-partner *every week*.

At Refuge, we've learned in our 37 years that what starts as a slap or shove can escalate into a pattern of frequent brutal beatings, and can even lead to death.

We've learned that far from being about *losing control*, domestic violence is actually about men *taking control*.

And we've learned that emotional abuse can do a huge amount of harm.

Forewarned is forearmed, so Refuge would like to alert you to some of the early warning signs of domestic violence.

- Is the man in your life charming one minute and terrifyingly aggressive the next?
- Is he excessively jealous and possessive?
- Is he stopping you from seeing your family and friends?
- Is he constantly criticizing you and putting you down in public?
- Does he control your money?
- Does he tell you what to wear, who to see, where to go, what to think?
- Does he pressure you to have sex when you don't want to?
- Are you starting to walk on eggshells to avoid making him angry?

Refuge

For women and children.
Against domestic violence.

Don't ignore the early warning signs. www.refuge.org.uk

Registered charity no: 277424

3. A poster encouraging women to report domestic violence

variation between 13 per cent of women reporting abuse in one city in Japan to 61 per cent of women in a province of Peru. It is estimated that a woman is beaten by her partner every fifteen seconds in America. In one survey 25 per cent of American women reported suffering domestic abuse at the hands of a partner. According to the UK Government 29.9 per cent of British women interviewed had experienced domestic abuse by a partner or family member since they were aged 16 and 17 per cent of men had.

Other statistics on domestic violence are revealing. An American study found that between 25 and 40 per cent of domestic violence cases start during the time the victim is pregnant. There are various theories over this connection, but perhaps the most convincing is that the abuser is seeking to regain control over the victim's body and affections, which he fears he is losing. Another important statistic is that women are attacked many times before they report the attacks to the police. In one UK study it was thirty-five times. This is significant when we look at the response of the police to domestic violence. Another important factor is that domestic violence does not end when a party leaves home. In one study 76 per cent of domestic violence victims who left home suffered continued violence.

Domestic violence and children

There is ample evidence of the negative impact on children of living in a house in which there is domestic violence. Children suffer emotional, financial, and educational harms. Many children feel they are to blame for the abuse. The impact of domestic violence on children is one of the reasons why domestic violence cannot be dismissed as simply a private matter, in which others should not be involved. One of the particularly tragic impacts of witnessing domestic abuse is that girls are more likely than on average to enter relationships with abusers, and boys are more likely to become abusers.

Causes of domestic abuse

There are three prominent theories of domestic abuse.

1. Emotional and psychological problems suffered by the abuser. These locate the cause of domestic abuse as within the abuser, citing anger management problems; or difficulties dealing with conflict. There is also a well-established link between alcohol and drug abuse and domestic violence.

2. Relational problems. Others see domestic abuse as not so much a problem about an individual but a reflection of a difficult relationship between the parties. Poor communication skills or volatile partnerships are to blame. This is a controversial approach, because it suggests that it is the fault of both the abuser and the victim that the violence has occurred.

3. The position of women in society. This approach tends to rely on theories of patriarchy: that men dominate women throughout society. This perspective argues that the general attitude towards women is reflected in domestic violence: men simply copy the behaviour expected and encouraged in society and society condones such behaviour. This can be supported by evidence which shows that violence often occurs when women do not fulfil their traditional roles and men use violent means to reassert their authority. US academic Elizabeth Schneider states:

> [H]eterosexual intimate violence is part of a larger system of coercive control and subordination; this system is based on structural gender inequality and has political roots...In the context of intimate violence, the impulse behind feminist legal arguments [is] to redefine the relationship between the personal and the political, to definitively link violence and gender.

The legal response to domestic violence

A much quoted statement by the jurist Hale, writing in the seventeenth century, suggested that a husband could beat his wife,

as long as he used a stick no wider than his thumb. This was part
of the traditional approach of the law that a father was in charge of
controlling his household and could use necessary force to do so. It
was not until the 1970s that the issue was brought to the attention
of the public, through the feminist movement. Erin Pizzey's book,
Scream Quietly or the Neighbours Will Hear, was particularly
influential. Effective legal responses in most Western countries did
not start until the late 1970s and even then these were limited.

The legal response to domestic violence can be broken down into
three broad categories:

- The criminal law. This involves proceedings brought by the state
  against the abuser. The remedies typically involve imprisonment
  or a community service order. In some jurisdictions courts can
  require an abuser to attend classes to address his or her behaviour.
- Civil proceedings. These are brought by the victim (or another
  person on behalf of the victim). The result of these proceedings
  are orders which are designed to protect the victim, rather than
  punish the abuser.
- Public law obligations. Some jurisdictions put obligations on local
  governments to provide services such as alternative housing, or
  shelters.

Criminal proceedings

A striking example of the law's failure to take domestic violence
seriously is the marital rape exemption, which applied in many
common law countries, including America and England. Two
reasons were given for why a husband could not be guilty of raping
his wife for two connected reasons. The first was that the law
supported the doctrine of unity, namely that on marriage the
husband and wife become one. Being one person, they could not
commit a crime against each other. The second is that it was
deemed that on marriage a wife gave irrevocable consent to her
husband having sex with her whenever he wished. It is astonishing

that these arguments were regarded as sufficient until relatively recently. The first US state to outlaw marital rape was South Dakota in 1975, and the last North Carolina in 1993. In England it was 1992, when the House of Lords overturned the traditional approach. Although most Western countries made marital rape a crime in the last few decades of the twentieth century, there are still many countries in the world where marital rape is not a crime.

Although the official line is that a criminal offence committed in the home is as much a crime as one committed in the street, it has not always worked out that way in practice. Too often in the past police were ready to dismiss domestic abuse as 'domestics' and so not proper criminal offences. Even where it was taken seriously by the police, the prosecution service often would not take it seriously and decide to drop the prosecution. This is especially so where the victim decided not to give evidence in support. Even if the case did reach the court, there was difficulty in proving beyond reasonable doubt what took place in an incident witnessed by only two people. And even if a conviction was found, all too often a reduced sentence was used. In many Western countries this problem has been recognized and steps have been taken to improve the legal response to domestic violence.

Perhaps the most controversial issue is whether a criminal prosecution should be brought in cases where the victim does not wish a prosecution to proceed. The traditional approach was that if the complaint was 'withdrawn' by the victim then the criminal prosecution should be stopped. That was for two reasons. First, it was thought highly unlikely that a jury would convict without the evidence of the victim. Second, it was reasoned that the victim's choice should be respected. However, that approach is under challenge. Criminal proceedings are generally brought by the state and by the victim of the incident. The victim, therefore, has no formal veto over whether the state should commence proceedings. Supporters of 'pro-prosecution' policies make a number of points. They argue that a victim's withdrawal of support for prosecution should be treated with a degree of suspicion. The victim may simply have been persuaded to withdraw her prosecution as a result of threats from her partner. Indeed requiring the prosecution to continue whether or not the victim's consent has been given may be seen as a way of discouraging the abuser from using threats in an attempt to stop the prosecution. It is also argued that even where the victim opposes the prosecution there may still be good reasons to pursue the prosecution, for example in order to protect the children or the interests of the state. The state may want to take a clear stand against intimate violence and a strong pro-prosecution policy can do that.

Opponents argue that there is a danger of the state compounding the abuse. If the police prosecute against the wishes of the victim of abuse, this infantilizes her. We should assume the woman knows what is best for herself, rather than assume we know better than her.

Some states in the US have tried mandatory arrest policies, most famously in Minneapolis, Minnesota. This led to a reduction in the rate of reported domestic abuse. However, there was much debate about whether this was because the policy discouraged domestic abuse, or discouraged people reporting the violence. Indeed in other places, including Omaha, Nebraska, the impact on the level of reported abuse was not significant.

Civil orders

Civil orders can be applied for by a victim of domestic abuse. These seek to prevent one party harassing or harming another. They can even be used to remove someone from their home. Orders preventing molestation are normally easy to obtain. Imagine being a lawyer seeking to argue that his client should be allowed to molest his partner! It's a difficult case to make. Hence when someone applies for one of these orders it is generally granted. On the other hand the removal of a person from their home is a major invasion of their rights and generally requires a strong justification.

Orders against molestation have been criticized from several angles. Men's groups have complained that they are easy to obtain, but once made the father is labelled an abuser and the fact the order was made can be brought up in further proceedings. In addition, women's groups have complained that non-molestation orders are used as a way of delaying a proper response to domestic violence. They suggest that a man who has abused his partner is, in effect, told not to do so again, rather than a proper legal response being provided. Supporters of the order emphasize that the orders can specify precisely what behaviour is unlawful and so make it quite clear to the parties what behaviour is or is not permitted.

One issue which arises is who should be able to apply for these civil orders. You might think anyone should be able to. If someone is harassing or molesting you, should you not be able to apply for an injunction to prevent them? The answer must be yes. But, the question is whether we want to have a different set of rules for domestic abuse cases from cases involving strangers. You might, if you think we should be more ready to grant an injunction in a case involving those in an intimate relationship than in other cases. That might be because you are concerned that allowing anyone who is bothered by someone else to sue is likely to lead to a vast number of claims. If you were minded to take everyone who bothered you to court to seek an order that they would never do it again, you would become very good friends with your lawyer, not to mention the court usher and the judge! There is, perhaps, another issue here, and that is that doing something that bothers someone else can be done by accident. Domestic abuse, however, is never accidental. The case detailed in Box 4 illustrates the problems.

Most jurisdictions draw a distinction between cases involving strangers and those involving people who are or have been in an intimate relationship. In English law, for example, only those who are in an 'associated relationship' (e.g. those who are relatives or have lived together) can apply for a non-molestation order. Where

> **Box 4 *DPP v King* (2000)**
>
> King had a brief conversation with a woman, C, who lived close to him. He decided he wanted to pursue a relationship. He later called at her address and gave her a plant. She refused the gift. Two weeks later he wrote a three-page letter to her. C was distressed by this and reported the matter to the police. He was prosecuted under the Protection from Harassment Act 1977. It was held that the offer of a gift could not constitute harassment, nor could the letter which was neither threatening nor abusive. However, it was also found that he had been rifling through her rubbish bins and removing discarded pieces of clothing. That was said to have crossed the line from attempted 'courting' to harassment.

the problem is one involving others they need to show a course of conduct. A single incident of molestation will be insufficient.

An order removing someone from their home is dramatic. The English judges have described these orders as 'draconian' and in most jurisdictions such orders are only available in the most serious cases. One option in some cases is to regulate the occupation. A husband might be restricted to the top floor of the house or excluded from the wife's bedroom, for example. The order can also require a person to avoid an area around the home. This would prevent a person terrifying someone by hanging around their home.

To some commentators, and in many jurisdictions, an important issue is the property rights of the couple. A case involving a couple who co-own a house but cannot live together is a very different thing from a case involving someone who has no property interest in the house and is trying to remove the owner from it. This sounds a fairly reasonable approach to take in theory. In practice it is more complex. This is because it is far from straightforward to determine whether a person has a legal interest in a property or not. But where a victim of domestic violence is seeking protection there seems something odd about the courts delving into the past to ascertain whether there is a claim under property law or not.

In most jurisdictions, including generally the US, no difference is drawn between whether an applicant for a protection order is married to the other party or not. Somewhat surprisingly English law draws a distinction between applicants who are married to the owner or in a civil partnership with them, and applicants who are not. It is easier for an applicant to obtain an order if they are married, and that order can be unlimited. This distinction was introduced because when the legislation was debated in Parliament a vociferous campaign was launched in the media by those who believed that giving married and unmarried applicants the same rights to seek domestic violence injunctions would undermine marriage. How leaving a victim of domestic violence without protection would uphold marriage is a mystery. I suppose the message to her would be, 'you should have married your abuser and then the law would help you', but is that really a good message to send?

Another interesting issue in this regard is the extent to which conduct is relevant. That may seem a surprising issue, but imagine this. A man has been abusing his wife and the children are being caused serious harm. The man has nowhere to live and no income, and the wife could move in with her parents who have a large house nearby. The court may accept that the order must be made separating the couple, but should it be the man or woman who leaves?

Human rights and domestic violence

Increasingly the debate over the law's response to domestic violence is seen in terms of human rights. In the past, rights arguments tended to be used by those alleged to be abusers, who argued that their right to respect for private and family life and right to their home meant that the court could not make an order removing them from the home. However, more recently human rights claims have been made by victims of violence that they have a human right to protection. Traditionally human rights arguments have been used to keep the state out and so rights have been 'negative', but the courts are now willing to accept a more positive understandings of rights, requiring the state to intervene to protect vulnerable people. This has led to an acknowledgement in the European Court of Human Rights that the state has a positive obligation to protect those suffering serious domestic abuse, even where they do not want assistance. The Istanbul Convention provides a European-wide convention on violence against women, including domestic violence. It states:

> Parties shall take the necessary legislative and other measures to adopt and implement state-wide effective, comprehensive and coordinated policies encompassing all relevant measures to prevent and combat all forms of violence covered by the scope of this Convention and offer a holistic response to violence against women.

The Convention goes on to detail ways in which signatory states are required to put in place policies to prevent and prosecute domestic abuse.

In American law although the courts have acknowledged that the Constitution protects marital privacy, that does not nowadays mean that violence goes without a remedy. Many states provide civil and criminal remedies to victims of domestic violence.

Conclusion

Although most Western systems have at last recognized that domestic violence is a major problem there is still a long way to go to produce an effective legal response. Of course, the law is only a small part of how society needs to respond to domestic abuse. Shelters for victims, public housing, and education are all needed. The home is still a dangerous place for women to be and everyone needs to work to change that.

Chapter 3
Divorce

One of the most striking changes in family life over the past forty years has been the increasing prevalence of divorce. If ever anyone got married utterly confident it would be for life, few do so now. Divorce has become commonplace. This is all the more surprising given the drop in marriage rates. It might be thought as fewer people now marry, only the most committed would do so and therefore the divorce rate would decline. That has not been so.

The likelihood of divorce

It is commonly said in the media that half of marriages are likely to end in divorce. However, such figures are typically arrived at by comparing the number of marriages and number of divorces. As the number of divorces in a given year is approximately half that of the number of marriages, it is easy to assume that there is a 50 per cent chance of a marriage breaking down. However, that is an erroneous assumption. There are several reasons why. First, the fact that the number of marriages has declined means that we cannot assume that because, in a given year, the number of marriages and divorces are the same, half the marriages entered into today will end in divorce. Second, no account is taken here of immigration and migration. Third, and most significantly, a large number of factors influence the likelihood of divorce. For example, the divorce rate for marriages where one party has married previously is far higher than cases where neither party has married before. Similarly age, religious beliefs, socio-economic background, and so forth can all play a significant role in the chances of a marriage breaking down. Perhaps the most reliable statistics on marital breakdown are those which look at the number of marriages in a particular year that have broken down fifteen years later. In the UK, 22 per cent of marriages in 1970 had ended in divorce by their fifteenth wedding anniversary, whereas 33 per cent of marriages in 1995 had ended after the same period of time. In the US 29 per cent of first marriages among women aged 15–44 were disrupted (ended in separation, divorce, or annulment) within ten years.

The statistics on divorce

In the UK there has been a fivefold rise in the divorce rate. Although, to be fair, the figures for the last few years have been dropping off. There were 119,589 divorces in 2010, as compared with 153, 282 divorces in 2009. The divorce rate (the number of divorces per 1,000 marriages per year) has risen from 4.7 in 1970 to 13.7 in 1999. In 2011 the divorce rate in England and Wales fell to 11.1 divorcing people per 1,000 married population. In the US the rates are lower, dropping from 4.0 in 2000 to 3.6 in 2010.

The picture of a rising divorce rate provokes different reactions. To the pressure group Marriage Today this is a disaster:

> The damage done by divorce is devastating. Research has proven that the damage of divorce on children not only lasts for a lifetime, but is also transferred to their children. Adults tell me that going through a divorce is worse than death.

Not only are there personal losses caused by divorce, it has been suggested that the cost of family breakdown on public finances is $112 billion in the US and £37 billion in the UK per year. Divorce may also be said to shake social stability by challenging the image of the family as comforting, secure, and enduring.

However, others are far less gloomy. Divorce may mark the release of the parties from an unhappy relationship. True, divorce may be a tragedy, but less of a tragedy than being stuck in an abusive relationship. The real sadness is that the relationship has come to an end, not that the law allows the parties to go their separate ways and try to find happiness in a new relationship.

Causes of divorce

Any government that was concerned by the divorce rate would want to know what causes divorce. Of course, there are multiple causes. We can refer to statistical links, which mean people in that group seem more likely to divorce than others. What we cannot say is what it is about being in a particular group that indicates divorce. Further, for all these groups, there are many marriages that survive without problems. The factors that are predictive of divorce include:

- Being married as a teenager
- Having previously been married
- Having lower educational achievement
- Having children from another partner
- Having had one's parents separate
- Living together before marriage

Some commentators find the causes of increased divorce in broader social changes. To some we are witnessing a change in attitudes towards marriage. Sociologist Antony Giddens has argued that people are no longer seeking 'the love of their life', but rather the perfect relationship. They will stay in a relationship for as long as it is fulfilling, but if it is not, they will seek out a better relationship. This is linked to the belief of some that society is becoming more individualistic, with people seeking out their own life plans and more reluctant to take on commitments to others.

Some have seen the rise in divorce as related to the changes in expectations about the role of women in society and family life. Women, in general, are less willing to accept a subservient role in marriage and expect a partnership of equals. Notably in Britain the large majority of divorce petitions are brought by women. In addition, it might be argued that increasing pressures at the workplace, for both men and women, make family life harder to fit in. Certainly the fact that it is now an economically viable option for women to live apart from their husbands has played a factor in the perceived feasibility of divorce.

Another point that should be made is that life expectancy impacts on marriage. It has been noticed that the average length of a marriage is similar today to what it was in the Victorian era. It is just that today divorce ends a marriage at the time when death would have done so in the past. So marriages are not necessarily shorter, it is the reason for their termination which is changing.

Perhaps the most controversial issue is the extent to which the law on divorce itself is to blame for increased divorce rates. Does the fact it is now easier to divorce cause more people to seek divorce? There is a sense in which the law on divorce must be connected with the divorce rate. If the law forbade divorce, the divorce rate would be zero! That would not mean that we would all have happy marriages, no doubt it would cause many 'empty shell marriages' where people would technically be married, but in reality have no real relationship. More seriously, there is debate over whether having a liberal law on divorce makes divorce more acceptable and therefore more common. It seems unlikely that it would. Most people do not seek out a lawyer to discuss divorce until the relationship has truly broken down. I suppose there might be the odd case where a person, believing the law would not allow divorce, would struggle on with their marriage, but there can be few people these days who remain in marriage because they think the law would not permit a divorce. They are likely to remain for religious or family reasons (e.g. the children), but these are pressures beyond the law.

The aims of divorce law

There is much dispute over what the aims of a divorce law ought to be. Some argue the law should seek to discourage divorce. It is unlikely that the law on divorce will discourage marital disharmony, but it might do more to save marriages. Some argue that divorce proceedings should be used as a time to offer marriage counselling and promote reconciliation. Indeed the English Family Law Act 1996 attempted to do this, encouraging those divorcing couples to make use of free marriage guidance, but studies suggested only a handful of marriages were thus saved. This is unsurprising. People do not turn to lawyers when the marriage first enters difficulties, but only when it is irreparable, often when one or other wishes to remarry. Indeed there is an argument that if the couple have reached the point of seeking divorce, encouraging reconciliation may not be sensible, especially if there has been domestic abuse.

Others would give divorce law a less grand aim: simply to lessen the bitterness. Sir Paul McCartney described his divorce as 'going through hell'. Many will be able to relate to that. There is no doubt that some divorce law systems seem designed to increase, not reduce bitterness. A person seeking a divorce on seeing a lawyer will be first asked to recall all the worst things about their marriage so that the divorce petition can be prepared. That seems hardly conducive to reducing ill will between the parties! On the other hand, not everyone sees the goal of reducing bitterness as unproblematic. It may be argued that bitterness is inevitable in a divorce. To pretend that the parties will have goodwill towards each other is demeaning to the parties and a failure to recognize their feelings. Indeed one English study found the major complaint of divorcing couples was that they had not had an opportunity to tell the judge all the horrible things the other party had done to them. Nevertheless, even if one agrees that the parties should have the chance to vent their feelings about the other and express their anger, it is far from clear that a courtroom is the best place. It is certainly not the cheapest!

Another goal, perhaps a surprising one, might be that divorce should not involve unnecessary expenditure for the state or parties. The point here is that if the couple are separating there are plenty of things that will need discussion, negotiation, and perhaps even judicial resolution: what should happen to the children, what will happen to property, etc. The actual granting of the divorce should not take so much effort or cost so much that the parties cannot concentrate on the more important issues, such as disputes over children.

The development of divorce

For most countries the history of divorce law has been a gradual liberalization of the law. In England the law on divorce was governed by the Ecclesiastical courts. Under the traditional church understanding although a marriage could be annulled in limited circumstances, divorce was not available. If you were very rich and influential you might be able to obtain an Act of Parliament to enable divorce or set up a new church to authorize the annulment of your marriage! The Matrimonial Causes Act 1857 opened the door to allow divorce, but only using highly restricted grounds, with it being much harder for a wife to obtain a divorce than a husband. Gradually there were minor liberalizations in divorce, but by the 1960s there was increasing acknowledgement that the law was inadequate. Ironically, perhaps, it was a report from the Archbishop of Canterbury, the head of the Church of England, which galvanized the UK government into action. The Archbishop's concern was that there were too many couples who had separated, but were unable to divorce, and some then started living with someone else. These 'empty shell marriages', and the resulting living together outside marriage, were demeaning the nature of marriage, he argued. The case for liberalizing divorce was, therefore, seen as a way of upholding the special status of marriage.

American laws varied from state to state but most until the late 1960s were fault based, requiring proof of adultery or cruelty. California became the first state to depart from a fault-based ground, introducing no-fault divorce in 1969. Many states then followed so that today all states have at least some element of no fault. The move to no fault was influenced in part by an acknowledgement that too often couples seeking a divorce were required to make up untrue grounds for a divorce and that the state should not be restricting the freedom of couples seeking a divorce.

Forms of divorce law

There are a number of ways different legal systems regularize divorce.

Fault-based grounds

The traditional model for a divorce law is to require proof of fault. Typically the fault-based ground relies on proof of adultery or unreasonable behaviour, such as violence. Those countries which have such grounds are not consistent in the extent to which these grounds must be proved. In England, although adultery and unreasonable behaviour need to be alleged, there is no need for them to be proved, except in rare cases where the divorce is defended. Indeed there is evidence that in some cases couples present petitions based on a wholly spurious set of grounds. In other jurisdictions, grounds need to be proved on the balance of probabilities. Supporters of fault-based divorce argue that the law should acknowledge the seriousness of divorce by requiring proof that there is a good enough reason to allow it.

No-fault ground

Some countries rely on a no-fault system of divorce. This simply requires one of the parties to request a divorce and there is no need for there to be proof of any misconduct. Most US states have no-fault grounds for divorce.

No-fault divorce is not without controversy, as Baroness Young has argued:

> The message of no fault is clear. It is that breaking marriage vows, breaking a civil contract, does not matter. It undermines individual responsibility. It is an attack upon decent behaviour and fidelity. It violates common sense and creates injustice for anyone who believes in guilt and innocence.

Some systems of no-fault divorce do require proof of marital breakdown, although there is no need to identify who is responsible for the breakdown. Another variation of no fault is when divorce is permitted even though one party objects to the divorce being granted.

Mixed system

England has a mixed system. Indeed it is a rather confusing mix of fault and no fault. The actual ground for divorce is irretrievable breakdown, which looks like a no-fault system. However the only way a party can show irretrievable breakdown is by proving one of five facts. These include fault-based grounds (e.g. adultery) and non-fault-based grounds (e.g. two years' separation and consent to divorce). In effect applicants can choose to go for a fault-based ground or a non-fault-based ground. As the fault ground does not require a set period of separation it tends to be the most commonly used.

'Drive-by divorce'

There has been support for divorce to become a bureaucratic procedure. A good example is that proposed by the UK Government in 2012, that divorce be performed through an internet hub. A party can log on and fill in the divorce petition online, claiming the marriage has broken down irretrievably. If the other party agrees, an administrator will produce a decree. That will undoubtedly be cheaper for couples, as no paperwork is involved; it will be less stressful because parties do not need to list the reasons for the breakdown; it will promote privacy; and save the judiciary for cases which really need the expertise of a judge. So what might be wrong with such an approach?

Some might claim that it trivializes divorce. If getting a divorce is slightly easier than buying a train ticket online, isn't that demeaning marriage? Divorce is a time of guilt, fear, and anguish. Shouldn't the law respond to a request for a divorce with the kind of solemnity that shows due respect for these emotions?

Another question is whether 'drive-by divorce' encourages people to divorce responsibly. Should we at least expect people to take time over their decision and make it after appropriate reflection? Supporters of a quickie divorce law might respond that people do not take the step to seek divorce from the law without heart-searching consideration. To tell people who seek a divorce to think carefully is deeply patronizing.

A more serious concern is whether the rights of the less affluent party in the divorce (usually the woman) will be protected if she is pressurized to settle and divorce quickly. At least in going to court her interests, and the interests of children, will be more adequately protected. Speeding through a divorce may mean that inadequate provision is made for women, especially if it means that time is not taken to ascertain the full extent of her husband's assets.

Perhaps concerns over the use of the internet trivializing divorce are all rather old-fashioned. The internet is used for all kinds of important transactions and requiring paper forms is outdated. Further, even accepting solemnity should mark a divorce, need this be done in expensive court rooms or using judges? Maybe religious services or secular parties could mark the passing of the marriage, if ceremony is what people need.

Conclusion

One of the lessons from the law on divorce is that there are limits to what the law can do. Its history shows that the law cannot stop marriages breaking up. Nor is it in a position to make an effective determination of who caused a relationship to come to an end. Most legal systems now seek to do more than record that a marriage has come to end. Perhaps that is the most we can expect of the law. Anything more may simply increase the bitterness the parties inevitably feel.

Chapter 4
Parents

What makes someone a parent? Consider Ben. He was born using donated sperm from Alfred and a donated egg from Carla. Dawn carried him under a surrogacy arrangement and handed him over to Edward and Fred, who raised him for five years together. Fred and Edward separated four years ago and Ben lives with Fred who is now living with Gloria, to whom Ben is very close. A reasonable case could be made for regarding Alfred, Carla, Dawn, Edward, Fred, or Gloria being Ben's parents. Their claims would essentially fall into one of three categories:

1. The genetic link. For some people the definition of a parent is straightforward: the mother is the person whose egg led to the production of the child and the father is the person whose sperm did. Parenthood is simply a matter of biology. Of course, it is only comparatively recently that we could rely on genetics as the basis of parenthood with any reliability. DNA tests now mean that we can discover who is genetically related. Previously, presumptions had to be relied upon, such as that the husband of a woman who gave birth was the father of the child. Of course such a presumption was unreliable, and indeed not always true. An unmarried father in the past would have struggled to prove he was the father of a child, but the scientific tests now provide him with a way of demonstrating his biological link with the child.

2. Care. For others what makes someone a parent is the care of the child. It is hours of cuddles, feeding, and washing which makes a parent, not the (possibly very casual) act of sexual intercourse leading to a child.

3. Intention. Some commentators have suggested that we should look at who was intended to be a parent by those involved in the creation of the child. So, a sperm donor is not a parent if it was never intended that he would be a parent by those involved in the child's creation. Similarly a partner of a person receiving treatment might be a parent if that is the intention, even though they are not biologically connected to the child. Those who intend to take on the responsibilities of parenthood should be recognized as being the parents.

It would be wrong to suggest that the law must adopt only one of these approaches. The current law in most jurisdictions is an uneasy mix between all of these. The father is normally the person whose sperm was used to create the child, but there is an exception in the case of sperm donors, who are not the father of any child, as long as they donate through a licensed clinic. In such a case the husband or partner (whether male or female) of the mother will be the father or other parent. American and English law might be said to be based on the premiss that a genetic parent is the legal parent, unless there is a very good reason not to apply that rule.

A middle path is also found in some jurisdictions by a distinction drawn between parenthood and parental responsibility. Parenthood is the official legal designation that someone is the parent of a child. Parental responsibility is the rights and responsibilities that a parent has. It is quite possible in English law, for example, for someone to be a parent, but not have parental responsibilities; or to have parental responsibilities, but not be a parent. To give one example, a step-parent can be given parental responsibility, even though they do not have the status of

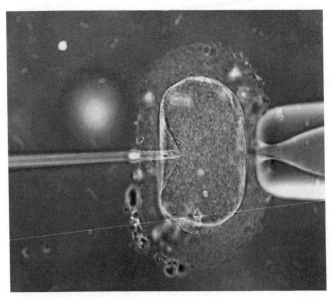

4. The moment of conception using IVF

a parent. This provides a way of the law recognizing the genetic and social link in different ways.

One important significance of the definition of parenthood is that under the genetic link a child will have one mother and one father. Traditionalists see it as beneficial for a child to have a contribution of a male and a female adult at the heart of their lives. To others, that demonstrates the greatest weakness of the genetic approach: it fails to acknowledge the diversity in family life. It means a same-sex couple will not be able to be parents together of a child. Further, it means a child cannot have more than two parents; even though many children will in fact have several adults who fulfil the role of parents. The care model means that the sex of the parents becomes irrelevant and there is no restriction as to the number of parents a child might have. Supporters of that model will claim it reflects how children experience parenthood. But some argue that if parenthood can define care it loses its certainty. How much care do you have to do in order to gain the title parent? What if you undertook care in the past, but do not now? And how is a third party (e.g. a doctor) to know whether you are a parent or not?

Arguments over parenthood might be resolved in several ways. One view would be that we should ask, who do children think are their parents? Children are, in fact, surprisingly flexible about parenthood and are happy to accept, for example, that they have two mothers or two fathers. It is society which has more difficulty accepting this than children themselves. If we were to look at the issue from the child's perspective, it may well be that the care model would be most accurate. However, it might not be that straightforward. Would a child cared for by a grandmother or nanny necessarily treat that grandmother or nanny as a parent? That may indicate that the marker of being a parent is not just any care, but a particular kind of care. But what would that be? Is it possible to identify in terms of the work done care that is uniquely parental? Does a child distinguish between the grandparent and the parent because that is what adults have told them to do? Or because the relationship between them is different?

Another approach one could take to the definition of parenthood is to consider what allocation of parenthood would best promote the child's welfare? The most natural response to this would be to suggest the person who is likely to make the best decisions for the child should be allocated parenthood. That will probably be the person who knows the child best and supports the care model.

But before you tie your colours to the care model mast, consider this. If we were to firmly reject the genetic model, is there a good reason why children should not be removed from their parents at birth and placed with whoever tops the list of those willing to adopt a child? Are we really sure that the child born to a single parent in a deprived area will not be better off cared for by a wealthy, well-educated couple who are offering care? Such a proposal is known as 'licensed parenting'. Few writers have been willing to go quite that far, but in a controversial book, James Dwyer, an American professor, has suggested that we can identify groups of parents (e.g. drug addicts, those with low IQ) where there is a good chance that if they raise a child the child will have to be taken into the care of the state, in which case why not remove them at birth and save the children the anguish?

The fact that most people find the model of licensed parenting not acceptable, even the more limited version of it, indicates that we do recognize that there is a special bond between biological parents and their children. Most parents feel an incredibly strong bond with their children from the moment of birth. That cannot be entirely put down to the caring relationship between them (see Box 5).

The issues also arise in relation to surrogacy. The case detailed in Box 6 gives a good example of the different ways the law can respond to surrogacy arrangements.

It is in the instance of lesbian parents where the law can face a particular difficulty. There have been quite a number of these cases coming before the courts. The lesbian couple ask a friend (often a gay man) to provide sperm they can use to produce a child. They do this informally (i.e. not through a licensed clinic). A child is born and disagreement breaks out among the adults. The man wants to play a significant role in the child's life, while the women wish to raise the child as their own, without any outside interference. Of course, in many cases the parties are able to resolve the disagreement between themselves. However, that is not always possible and sometimes a court order is sought.

Box 5 *Re B (A Child) (2009)*

Harry (not his real name) was born to a couple who were unable to look after him. His grandmother undertook his care. Four years later his father's life had become much more settled and he was keen to take Harry into his care. He was assessed in an expert report to offer 'good enough' (i.e. adequate) parenting. Another report assessed that Harry's current care with the grandmother was excellent and likely to continue to be. In the lower courts the view was taken that the case involved a natural parent who was able to offer adequate care for a child. A very strong case was therefore required to prefer an alternative carer. The UK Supreme Court took a different line. The case should simply be decided on what was best for the child. The choice was between the 'excellent' care of the grandmother or the 'good enough' care for the father. The grandmother must be preferred. The court also noted that while it was true that, generally speaking, children were best cared for by their parents, a court must focus on what is best for the particular child in the case.

Box 6 *In re Baby M* (1988, New Jersey)

A surrogacy contract was entered into between Mrs Whitehead and Mr Stern (who was married to another woman). The agreement was that Mr Stern would pay Mrs Whitehead $10,000 and in return Mrs Whitehead agreed to become pregnant using Mr Stern's sperm, and hand the child over to him immediately after the birth. She did hand the child (Melissa) over, but four days later changed her mind and took the child and refused to return it.

Under New Jersey law (as in most states) the legal position was that Melissa's mother was Mrs Whitehead and her father was

(continued)

Box 6 Continued
presumed to be Mr Whitehead. The New Jersey lower court gave effect to the agreement, terminated Mrs Whitehead's parental status, and allowed the Sterns to adopt the child. However, the Supreme Court invalidated the surrogacy and required the lower courts to determine who should be given custody based on best interests. This assessment later meant that Melissa lived with the Sterns but with regular visitation with Mrs Whitehead.

One option is to emphasize the central family unit provided by the couple and suggest that nothing must disrupt the stability provided by them. The man might be permitted to see the child occasionally so that they know who their father is, but otherwise he should be regarded as a 'secondary parent'.

Disputes between parents

When parents separate there are often disputes over the children. These tend to centre on three issues:

- Where the child's primary residence will be
- How regularly the child will have contact with the other parent
- Disputes over the upbringing of the child

So how does the court decide disputes over children? The short answer is simple: the court will decide what will be in the welfare or best interests of the child. This is the approach taken in America, England, and most countries. Of course, that raises as many questions as it answers. What is the welfare of the child?

In the UK, the Children Act 1989 contains a list of factors the judge can take into account when considering welfare:

(a) the ascertainable wishes and feelings of the child concerned (considered in light of his age and understanding);

(b) his physical, emotional, and educational needs;

(c) the likely effect on him of any change in his circumstances;

(d) his age, sex, background, and any characteristics of his which the court considers relevant;

(e) any harm which he has suffered or is at risk of suffering;

(f) how capable each of his parents, and any other person in relation to whom the court considers the question to be relevant, is of meeting his needs;

(g) the range of powers available to the court under this Act for the proceedings in question.

These factors do not, of course, tell the judge what orders will promote a child's welfare, but do give some elements to consider.

Not surprisingly, the welfare principle has received more than its fair share of critics. It is said to be hopelessly vague, leaving the judge with a broad discretion which will simply reflect the prejudices of the particular judge. Consider, for example the case detailed in Box 7.

Critics of the welfare principle claim that a case like this, and there are plenty more examples, show how what a judge decides

Box 7 *Re W (Residence Order)* [1999]

The parents of two children had separated. The children lived with the mother and her new male partner. They adopted a naturist lifestyle and were often naked in front of the children. The father objected and took the matter to the court. The judge at first instance agreed with the father that the behaviour was objectionable and ordered the parents to refrain from being nude in front of the child. The Court of Appeal disagreed, holding that parents around the country held a range of views on naturism and it could not be said the parents were behaving improperly.

is or is not good for a child is simply a matter of their own view. The law is unpredictable and depends on the luck of which judge you happen to be before. Worse, it can mean the law gives force to the prejudices of the judge. It is not difficult to look back on cases heard a couple of decades ago which purported to be made in the best interests of the child, but in fact reflect the prejudices of the judiciary against women, same-sex couples, or atheists.

Another concern is that the test does not give enough weight to the rights of parents to raise their children as they see fit. American law seems more deferential to parents' assessment of welfare than other jurisdictions (see Box 8).

Box 8 *Troxel v Granville* (2000)

A dispute arose between paternal grandparents and the mother of the children following the death of the children's father. The grandparents wished to have increased visitation rights. The mother wished to limit these to one short visit a month and visits on special holidays. The grandparents succeeded in the lower courts which increased visitation rights, saying that was in the best interests of the child. However the State of Washington Supreme Court and the US Supreme Court held that the Washington statute which allowed any person to petition for visitation rights was unconstitutional because it interfered with parental decision making. The parent had the right to determine the appropriate visitation rights of non-parents. There has been much dispute over the extent to which the court has left open the power of the courts to override a parental decision based on the best interests of the child. One reading is that if a parent is deemed fit their decision about a child's upbringing cannot be interfered with. But that may be reading too much into the decision.

Judicial prejudice is an undoubted disadvantage of the welfare principle, but any approach which was based on a rule-based system would carry its own disadvantages. The benefit of asking the judge to focus on the welfare of the particular child is that it enables her or him to produce a result which is tailored to the particular needs of the child. It recognizes that each child is different and each family is different. Presumptions based on what is generally good for children or what is normal are of little use to a judge seeking to produce the result which is best for the child before the court. This is particularly because the kinds of case which come to the court are not average or normal cases.

Ultimately much will depend on the faith you have in the judiciary. If you are persuaded that generally they have the wisdom and experience, backed up by the provision of expert evidence, to determine the result which will work best for children, you will favour the welfare principle. If, however, you are suspicious of judges and wish to trim back their discretion you may prefer a set of clear legal presumptions that should be followed unless there is clear evidence to the contrary.

One other aspect of the welfare/best interests principle is worth bringing out. It requires the judge to make the order based on what is best for the child. The interests of the parents or other adults are not to be taken into account. The test requires the judge to make the order which will be best for the child even if it will be unfair or inconvenient for the parents. This, it is suggested, is entirely appropriate. Children will be the most vulnerable people in the case of family break up. They will lack the financial, social, and emotional resources to deal with the consequences, as compared with the adults. Further if there is blame to be placed for the family break up it does not lie at the feet of the child. The judge should keep the child at the focus of the court's attention because, although the adults are likely to address the court, the child will often not be present.

It might, however, be questioned whether the prioritization of children's interests might go too far. Imagine a judge is faced with the option of making one of two orders. Order A is very slightly better for the child than Order B but will be disastrous for one of the parents. The welfare/best interests principle suggests that we should make Order A, but is that right? There may be a way around that if we argue that the notion of best interests need not be understood in an entirely selfish way. It is not good for children to be raised in relationships which demand unreasonable sacrifices of their parents.

Residence

Until recently the standard model for separating couples was that children should have 'primary residence' with one parent, typically the mother, but would then have regular contact (it used to be called access) with the other, typically the father, say one day a week or one weekend a fortnight. This standard model has come under challenge from a range of perspectives, leading to calls for presumption in favour of shared residence, where a child will spend a roughly equal amount of time with each parent. Fathers' groups, in particular, have argued in favour of this approach, believing that the standard model often discriminates against men.

A presumption in favour of shared residence is not a realistic starting point. First, research from Australia which sought to give support to this presumption, showed children often suffered considerable disruption moving regularly from house to house and sometimes even school to school. The solution of shared residence may seem fair from an adult perspective, but often is not best for the child. Second, shared residence is only a realistic possibility if both parents live close to each other and have a spare room. That, for many families, is a pipe dream. Third, there is something a little ironic in the fact that while women undertake the vast majority of childcare, fathers' groups complain that this is reflected in computing hours of care after relationship breakdown.

Visitation/contact

Normally the most contentious issue among separating couples is the extent of visitation/contact which the 'non-resident parent' (i.e. the parent with whom the child is not living) should have. This is often presented in gender terms as it is the father who is normally not resident with the child.

There are three major issues. The first is when the court should make an access contact order. Some jurisdictions operate on the basis that the child has a right of contact with both parents or that a parent has a right of contact with their child. Another option is to say there is a presumption that contact is in the welfare of the child. Under either system, if there is evidence that the contact will cause harm to the child then contact will not be ordered. In most jurisdictions it is very rare for some form of contact not to be ordered. For example, in England in 2011 there were 111,302 applications for a contact order heard and in only 333 were contact orders refused. Although judges are sometimes presented by the media as being keen to exclude men from their children's lives, this is an unfair complaint. The second issue, and more problematic, is the enforcement of the contact order. The problem is straightforward. Imagine the court has decided that a child should live with his mother and the mother must allow the father to see the child once a week, but the mother refuses. What is a court to do? The most extreme option would be to imprison the mother (no doubt after one or two warnings of what would happen if disobedience continued). After all that is what normally happens to someone who disobeys a court order. But such a course of action is hardly likely to promote the child's well-being. Indeed the child is likely to perceive the situation to be that her father has had her mother sent to jail and so damage future chances of happy contact. Other courses of action for refusing to allow contact with the father might include fining the mother or requiring her to undertake unpaid work. These too might harm the child and do not of themselves promote contact.

Indeed, the problem is that forced contact is unlikely to be productive. Contact between a child and non-resident parent is hard enough to maintain at the best of times, and where one parent believes the contact is undesirable it is unlikely to be effective. The better solution is to target the root of the problem: why do so many mothers refuse to allow contact? The answer, research suggests, is that they are fearful that they or their child will be the victim of (further) abuse. Nearly all cases of hotly disputed contact involve allegations of domestic abuse. The judge may well have decided that the past misconduct of the father is not a sufficient reason to deny contact. We do know that there are some cases where, even though contact has been ordered or agreed, abuse has continued. This makes these decisions agonizing: do we ignore the mother's fear, force contact, and run the risk of ongoing abuse? Or do we take heed of the mother's concerns and end effective contact between the child and father? Neither option is palatable. It may be that in some cases ordering that all contact between the father and child be supervised by a social worker is a solution, but that only seems workable in the short term.

It may be that through electronic media, texts, Skype, and the like, a child can keep contact with one parent, without the other parent having to be involved. Especially with older children this might be an acceptable option until the child is able, independently, to establish a relationship with the other parent. Some might say this kind of indirect contact is a poor substitute for proper face-to-face contact. But maybe, especially with teenagers, face-to-face contact is a false aspiration anyway. Even in intact families, parents don't typically spend whole days together with their teenager, and communication primarily through texts is not unknown.

Other issues

Courts can be faced with a wide range of other issues ranging from children's religious upbringing and disputes over medical treatment to cases about the surname a child should have. Boxes 9 and 10 detail good examples of the difficult issues that can arise.

Conclusion

This chapter has raised some complex issues. The definition of parenthood has become profoundly difficult. Maybe the time has come to move away from a debate over who is or who is not a parent to acknowledging that a range of adults have an important part to play in the life of a child and we need to recognize them. That need not be by calling them all parents, but giving some legal recognition to their significance. The chapter has also showed how notions of children's best interests and who is to decide what is in a child's welfare are hotly contested.

One welcome move in most legal systems is that parenthood is

Box 10 *Re G (Children)* (2012) (UK Court of Appeal)

The case involved three girls and two boys. The parents separated. A key issue was over their religious upbringing. While both parents were Jewish the father belonged to the Chassidic community which had strict regulations concerning every aspect of a person's life. The mother was less strict, but still an observant Jew. Munby LJ acknowledged that the courts normally did not wish to choose between religious beliefs. However, in this case there was no getting away from the issue. The child could not realistically follow the strict observance of the father and the mother's more relaxed observance at the same time. Munby LJ emphasized that welfare had to be understood in a broad sense and was about finding a good life for the child. This had to be understood by the values of a twenty-first-century parent which would include recognizing equality of opportunity between boys and girls; fostering and facilitating aspiration; and bringing a child to adulthood in a way that means the child can lead the kind of life they wish. The mother's way of life offered this to a greater extent than the father's.

no longer simply seen as about giving an adult rights over a child, but involves an acknowledgement they have important responsibilities too.

Chapter 5
Children's rights

The definition of childhood

The definition of childhood is a matter of dispute. Article 1 of the UN Convention on the Rights of the Child defines a child as any human being below the age of 18. However, many countries use different ages for different purposes. In American and English law 10, 13, 16, 18, and 21 are all used as significant ages for different legal purposes. This sometimes leads to some bizarre results, such as that under English law at 16 someone is old enough to sleep with their Member of Parliament, but not vote for them. In the US a person is mature enough at 16 to handle a car, but not a glass of beer until 21.

The UN Convention on the Rights of the Child has been ratified by most countries, although notably not by the United States. It protects a broad range of rights, including the following:

- The right that children's best interests be a primary consideration in all actions concerning children (article 3)

- The right to life (article 6)

- The right of a child 'who is capable of forming his or her own views...to express these views freely in all matters affecting the child' (article 12)

At one time the idea that children had rights was laughable. They were, infamously, to be seen but not heard. However, it has now become common to refer to children's human rights.

It is worth early on distinguishing between moral and legal rights. Just as there is a difference between law and morality—something may be legal but immoral (for example I can spread unpleasant rumours about my brother, but that would not be illegal)—so too there is a difference between a legal right and a moral right. To give one example, a person may believe that a child has a right to be loved by their parents. That is likely to be a claim of a moral right. A parent who does not love their child is breaking the child's moral right to be loved and the duty imposed upon the parent as a result. However, it is unlikely that loving your child could be a legal right: how could that right be enforced in the law? The notion of love is too vague.

Do children have rights? Although this is one of the most hotly disputed questions in family law, at one level the answer is obvious. They clearly do have the right to life, the right not to be tortured, etc. The real dispute is whether they have *all* the rights that adults do. Do they have the right to decide how to live their life? Or at least a limited version of that right? And do they have rights that adults do not have, such as the right to education? The debate over children's rights was ignited by a lively group of writers in the 1970s, who became known as the 'kiddie libbers' or, more prosaically, the child liberationists.

The child liberationists

Americans John Holt and Richard Farson were among those arguing in the 1970s that children need to be liberated from childhood. For them, childhood was a kind of 'modern slavery' which enables parents to control children as 'super-pets'. By undervaluing children's capabilities and presenting them as vulnerable the law allowed adults, and especially parents,

5. Do children have a right to refuse to eat broccoli?

to control children and deny them their rights. They called
for children to be given exactly the same rights as adults
(see Figure 5).

Their campaign never entered the political mainstream. In part
this was because their writing coincided with a growing
awareness of child abuse. Their calls to, for example, regulate
child sexuality in the same way as adult sexuality could too

readily be interpreted as a paedophile's charter. Fears over child crime and anti-social behaviour meant making school voluntary seem a dangerous proposal. Few children's rights supporters nowadays would present their claims as straightforward child liberationists.

Age discrimination

A more modern form of child liberationism might put the argument in terms of age-discrimination. Laws which treat those under 16 or 18 as different from other people are making assumptions about their capacity. They are assuming that those under 16 cannot make sensible decisions for themselves. Let's take the law on drinking alcohol, for example. In most countries a person cannot buy, or consume, alcohol until they reach a certain age, typically between 16 and 21. This is normally justified on the basis that until that age they will not understand the issues around alcohol and be able to make thoughtful decisions on the issue. But that is to make an assumption about someone based on their age. A 14-year-old could be far more knowledgeable about alcohol than an adult. Is making the assumption that all those under a certain age lack mental capacity to make a decision any more acceptable than it would be to assume that all those over 80 lacked capacity? Most people would certainly regard that as ageist. If we treat making assumptions about people based on their age as analogous to making assumptions about people based on their sex or race that means those who seek to use age as a criterion for capacity need to provide us with a good reason why its use can be justified. So how might child discrimination be justified?

One argument is that we need to restrict people doing things which will cause them or others harm if they do not understand sufficiently what they are doing. We could use an individualized test and assess the capacity for everyone who comes forward to buy alcohol, have sex, or vote. That is simply unrealistic.

Queues at bars would be even longer if every customer were to undergo a quick multiple choice test on the evils of alcohol. Using, say, the age of 18 provides a rough and ready, and practical, test of capacity. There may be unfairness to the precocious alcohol-loving 17-year-old, but that is a price worth paying to make life workable.

The law has to draw artificial boundaries so that the law can operate effectively. A good example is speed limits. On a road with a 30 mph speed limit, the truth is that a person going at 29 mph is probably no safer than someone going at 31 mph. However, the speed limit must be set at some level, even though comparing cases just either side of the line will look odd. Nevertheless, as long as we decide some restriction on speed is appropriate a workable law must put up with such arbitrariness and seek to select a speed which approximates to the level at which the speed becomes dangerous. Similarly with age. The age at which sexual relations becomes lawful may be 16, but no one believes that the stroke of midnight on one's birthday magically gives one the knowledge and maturity one needs to consent to sex. It is just that the law believes this is a pretty good marker of the age when that will occur.

This argument will not convince everyone. Discrimination is often justified on the basis it makes things easier. But we would not accept sex or race discrimination simply on the basis of the fact it would be more convenient. One response is to suggest that childhood age discrimination is not as bad as race or sex discrimination: everyone suffers it at some point in their childhood and they only need to wait a while and the discrimination is gone. That cannot be said for race or sex discrimination.

Another response would be to query the bureaucracy issue and argue that it exaggerates the potential problem. We could enable children to obtain a card from their doctor or a panel which confirms their capacity to engage in a particular activity. So the idea of the bartender quizzing children is not the only way to deal with ascertaining capacity. We could provide a workable scheme for mature children to prove their abilities and have a card allowing them to engage in activities.

There is one aspect of this debate that sometimes goes unrecognized. If, in order to avoid age discrimination, we moved from an age-based criterion to engage in these activities to a capacity-based criterion, what impact would this have on adults? It would mean that some adults would 'lose out'. A 22-year-old is currently assumed to have the capacity to buy alcohol or vote. However, a 22-year-old with learning difficulties might fail to pass the test needed. In liberating children, we might be depriving some adults of their freedom. Or would we? If a 22-year-old does not understand the issues around alcohol should they be free to buy it?

A moderate version of children's rights?

A more persuasive argument in favour of restricting children's rights may be made on the basis that restricting children's autonomy during childhood is necessary in order to maximize children's autonomy when they reach adulthood. The point is this. If we allowed 7-year-olds to decide for themselves not to go to school, we might be respecting their autonomy at that age. However, when those children reach adulthood, their range of choices, and therefore their autonomy, would be severely limited.

This has led to a popular approach, championed by writers such as John Eekelaar and Michael Freeman, which focuses on a child having an 'open future': reaching adulthood with a broad range of choices about how to live their life in the future. Developing this approach John Eekelaar refers to three interests that children have:

- Basic interests: these are the interests we have in the essential things in life

- Development interests: these are what are needed to develop the necessary social and educational skills
- Autonomy interests: the interests in children making decisions for themselves

Eekelaar suggests that although all these interests should be supported, where there is a clash, basic or developmental interests should win out over autonomy interests. The impact of such an approach would be that children are able to make decisions for themselves, but not if doing so would interfere with their basic or development interests. So a child would not be able to make a decision which caused serious ill health or seriously impeded their educational development. However, a child would be able to make decisions which did not affect the other interests, such as what clothes to wear. This kind of middle-ground approach may be summarized by saying that children should be encouraged to make decisions for themselves, but not if doing so causes clear present or future harm. That way we bring children to the brink of adulthood with a broad range of options, and experienced at making decisions.

There are some difficulties with this more moderate account of children's rights. One is how 'open' should the child's future be? If parents raise the child with a particular cultural identity, that may close off for them a range of cultural identities when they are older. Is it very wrong to raise a child with a strong sense of being Welsh? Or Muslim? Or atheist? The logical conclusion of the 'open future' argument is that children should be raised with an awareness of all cultures and religions and so choose for themselves which they wish. That, however, may be impossible for parents and arguably confusing for children. Further it would be hard for religious and cultural groups to operate without including youngsters in their activities. Perhaps we have to accept that raising children in families will inevitably shape the children and there is nothing wrong with that, as long as the children feel free to depart from their upbringing when they are old enough.

A similar point is that nowadays if children are to excel they need to specialize at an early age. A child who is seeking to excel in music, sports, or academia will inevitably focus on those activities at the expense of other activities. Is there anything very wrong in that? Surely not. Again that leads us to question the idea of the child with the open future. Perhaps a more realistic goal is that a child reaches adulthood with an acceptable range of options.

Opponents of children's rights

Not everyone is supportive of the argument that children should have rights. Paternalism is one basis of opposition to children's rights. It argues, contrary to the liberationist perspective, that children are far more vulnerable than adults. They lack the physical, mental, emotional, and social skills and resources that adults have. In short, they lack the capacity to make the kind of reasoned, rational decisions that deserve respect. Although children need protection, they do not need rights, because rights carry the danger of giving too much weight to the decisions they make. If we look at the position of children in the world today and see the poverty, abuse, and neglect that they all too often suffer, our response must be to offer protection, rather than choice. As we have seen, that claim will be denied by some who claim that children are far more knowledgeable and sophisticated than we give them credit for. Most parents readily accept their children are more adept with modern technology and more streetwise than they are. Further, as we have seen, there is an argument that these assumptions can be no more than generalizations and each person should be assessed in their own right.

A rather different response to the argument for paternalism and one heard less often is that adults are far more vulnerable and lacking capacity than we give ourselves credit for. In short, it is not that the current law underestimates children, it is that it overestimates adults.

Another criticism of rights comes from the writing of Onora O'Neill, who argues that the focus should be on duties that adults owe children, rather than the rights that children have. Rights supporters will immediately want to say that rights beget duties and indeed it is the duties that give rights their effectiveness. It might, therefore, be that O'Neill is making more a point about how the issue is presented than the substance of the claim. But there is more to O'Neill's point than one might realize. She explains that our obligations are broader than might be captured by a right. Our obligations to care, nurture, and cherish our children are important, but not neatly captured by a corresponding right.

A slightly different argument is that rights are inappropriate for the kind of family arrangements in which typically children are raised. Rights generally work in relation to claims against the government and to keep people out. They elevate values such as bodily integrity, privacy, and autonomy. But these are individualistic values. They are of less value in family life where concepts of mutuality and the attitudes of the parties to each other are crucial. In family life, at least if it is working well, the parties work together for the good of the family unit, and don't assert rights against each other. Love is what holds the family together, not a balancing of competing rights. Setting aside your own interests for the good of the family, and the idea of give and take which is so central to family life, will be undermined if the parties start to see themselves as having rights against each other. I find this a very convincing argument. However, it is just as true for adults as it is for children. It provides an argument against allowing anyone rights, rather than specifically children. Or, more convincingly, it argues for a form of rights which is based on relational, rather than individual interests.

Extra rights for children?

So far we have been considering whether there is a case for saying that children should not have all the rights that adults have. A case can be made that children should have special rights that adults do not have. This might include the right to receive goods which we normally expect adults to get for themselves, for example, a right to food and shelter. There may also be rights to protection from particular forms of harm that befall children. It might be argued that child sexual abuse is a particular kind of wrong different from adult sexual abuse. There may also be rights due to special needs that children have. The right to education would be the most obvious example.

Children's rights in the law

Many countries have been rather reluctant to explicitly recognize children's rights. This is not to say that their law does not protect children's rights. Most have laws requiring the provision of education; protecting children from sexual abuse and the like. Anglo-American law tends to emphasize the best interests and welfare of children, rather than their rights. While a child's views can be taken into account in determining their welfare, they are not, necessarily, determinative (see Box 11).

Family Law

Box 11 *Prince v Massachusetts* (1944)

The Supreme Court of the United States held that the government is entitled to interfere in the decisions that parents make if that is necessary in the interests of the child. Sarah Prince was a minister of the Jehovah's Witness faith and aunt and custodian of Betty M. She took her child to the streets to preach and was charged under child labour laws under which no girls under 18 were permitted to sell literature or other goods on a public thoroughfare. Sarah Prince challenged the legality of these offences. The Supreme Court upheld the law restricting the use of children in the sale of literature. It confirmed that while the law respects parental authority, the state can restrict it if necessary in the child's welfare. The court explained:

The family itself is not beyond regulation in the public interest, as against a claim of religious liberty. And neither the rights of religion nor the rights of parenthood are beyond limitation ... The right to practice religion freely does not include the right to expose the community or the child to communicable disease or the latter to ill-health or death ...

Parents may be free to become martyrs themselves. But it does not follow they are free, in identical circumstances, to make martyrs of their children before they have reached the age of full and legal discretion when they can make that choice for themselves.

Box 12 *Gillick* v *W Norfolk and Wisbech AHA* (1985)

Victoria Gillick, a Roman Catholic, challenged the legality of a Government notice that in 'exceptional circumstances' a doctor could give contraceptive advice to a girl under 16 without parental consent or consultation. She had five daughters under 16 and complained the notice was unlawful. The case went to the House of Lords where the majority accepted that if a doctor decided that it was in the best interests of an under-16-year-old that she be given the contraceptive advice she sought and that she was competent to understand the issues involved, then the doctor was permitted to provide the treatment without obtaining the consent of the parents first. This was a hugely important decision because it recognized that under-16-year-olds had the right to give effective legal consent to medical treatment.

In English law the leading case is that shown in Box 12. While the decision might appear to be a victory for children's rights, it is not that straightforward. Their Lordships emphasized that the competent child could only consent to treatment which a doctor thought was in her best interests. Further, later decisions held that although a competent child had the right to consent to treatment, it did not follow she had the right to refuse treatment. In the light of these cases the decision appears soundly based on a welfare assessment rather than a best interests assessment.

This last point raises a major problem for child rights advocates. There is a real danger that children's rights, if acknowledged, will only be given effect to when adults think it sensible. Or even worse, that they will only be given effect when it is in the interests of adults. This is a real danger because rarely are children in a position to enforce rights themselves. Their rights are nearly always enforced by adults. While this is not a 'knock down' argument against children's rights, it shows the danger that all too easily they can be used to undermine children, not enable them.

Conclusion

It is likely that we will hear more and more about children's rights in the years ahead. Rights have developed as powerful tools to make claims in courts and against government. The difficulty will be in developing a system of legal rights which will protect children from harm, but also recognize their right to self-determination. Further, it will be necessary to find a system of rights that recognizes the wonder and innocence of childhood, while protecting children from those who wish to devalue them.

Chapter 6
Child abuse

The problem of child abuse

A toddler is brought to hospital severely bruised. The parents say the boy fell down the stairs and, anyway, he is always running around and falling over. An expert paediatrician concludes that the bruises were caused by the parents abusing the child and could not be caused by rough and tumble play. A second opinion is called for and this paediatrician is less sure. There may well be abuse, but they think it is possible this was a result of an accident. Do we remove the child from the parents and take the child into care, aware that we might be imposing the harshest imaginable injustice on the parents and cause great harm to the child? Or do we risk leaving the child with the parents, aware that we may be leaving the child to face continued abuse? The stakes could hardly be higher.

It is often only in hindsight that we can tell what was the right thing to do. Most countries can point to cases where a child was left by social workers, who investigated concerns but decided not to intervene, and as a result the child died. But there are also cases where the local authorities intervened, only for it later to be discovered that an error was made. Consider the heart-breaking case detailed in Box 13.

Box 13 *Webster v Norfolk CC* [2009] [English Court of Appeal]

Mr and Mrs Webster had three children in three years. In late 2003 their middle child, B, was taken to hospital suffering multiple fractures. The hospital and local authority assessed the injuries to be non-accidental and caused by his parents. The children were taken into care and adopted by late 2005.

In 2006 Mrs Webster became pregnant again. In the course of care proceedings relating to the new baby the Websters obtained fresh expert evidence in relation to B. The new report was powerfully of the opinion that the injuries to B were caused by scurvy and iron deficiency rather than abuse. At the initial assessment of abuse, scurvy was considered as not possible in the West and had not been considered as an explanation for the injuries. As a result of this new evidence, the care proceedings in relation to the baby were discontinued. The parents then sought to set aside all the orders relating to their three other children.

The Court of Appeal held that only in exceptional cases can an adoption order be overturned. There was nothing in the procedure that led to the making of the order which rendered the procedure flawed, and hence the adoption order could not be set aside. Wilson LJ emphasized that the children had been with the adopters for four years in an arrangement they had been told was permanent and the children were fully settled into their new life.

To make these decisions even harder, we cannot be sure that taking a child into care is doing just that. Too often public care has turned out to be abusive itself. The removal of the child by officials is one of the greatest powers a government has. And this power must be exercised with great caution. Social workers in many countries have received bad press. They are either seen as over-interventionist or as failing to do their job and not protecting children. Too often it is inadequate funding, poor management, and low morale which causes the problems.

A further issue is that while much emphasis is placed on responding to cases of suspected child abuse, less effort has been put into preventing abuse arising. There is widespread evidence that child abuse is most prevalent in families marked by poverty, mental health issues, and interpersonal problems. In Julia Brophy and Martha Cover's study, 84 per cent of parents in England who had children involved in care proceedings were dependent on public welfare payments. It would not, however, be correct to assume that poverty causes child abuse. There is no abuse in most low-income families. It may be that child abuse is more easily discovered among families with extensive use of public services. It may also be that the care proceedings involving neglect reflect difficulty in making provision for children, rather than maliciousness (see Figure 6).

The definition of child abuse

The definition of child abuse is problematic. Here is a popular one:

> Child abuse consists of anything which individuals, institutions, or processes do or fail to do which directly or indirectly harms children or damages their prospects of safe and healthy development into adulthood. (UK Department of Health, 1995)

This is a surprisingly wide definition. Letting a child eat too much chocolate would fall into this definition. But it is interesting that the definition is not restricted to individuals, but acknowledges that institutions and processes can cause child abuse. Pollution, poverty, and inadequate education can constitute significant setbacks for children. While abuse is commonly thought of in terms of sexual or physical abuse, in fact neglect constitutes the largest portion of child abuse in most countries. Further, looking

You know me. I live next door.
You know me. Dirty and hungry.
You know me. I'm always left alone.

You know me. Help.

When you think a child needs help,
talk to us. We're here 24/7. It's free
and you don't have to say who you are.
Call **0808 800 5000** or visit
nspcc.org.uk/helpline

NSPCC
HELPLINE
0808 800 5000
help@nspcc.org.uk

6. An NSPCC poster informating people about child abuse

at physical or sexual abuse, it is notable that much abuse is
committed by children on children.

One complex issue in relation to child abuse is the extent to
which the law should be sympathetic towards cultural
explanations for behaviour. Consider, for example, the case
detailed in Box 14.

The rates of child abuse are somewhat disputed, but there is no avoiding the grim picture. In America 3.3 million reports of child abuse are made a year, involving 6 million children. Every day five American children die as a result of abuse. A well-respected British charity (the National Society for the Prevention of Cruelty to Children) claims that 25.3 per cent of children have suffered some severe maltreatment during childhood. In both countries where there is abuse, the majority is committed by parents or guardians.

Legal responses to child abuse

The law has found it difficult to respond to the issue of child abuse. One difficulty is proof. As a leading English judge complained, courts have to 'penetrate the fog of denials, evasions, lies and half-truths which all too often descends' *(Lancashire CC v B* (2000)). Given abuse is often behind closed doors, it can be all but impossible to prove.

Even where the facts are known, the law's difficulties are not over. A key issue is how much harm is required before public intervention is deemed necessary. How much discretion do you leave parents? Or do children's rights to protection trump any parental rights? Take, for example, the issue of unhealthy diets. If a local authority discovers a child is obese, having been fed unhealthy food by the parents, what should be done? Is it just to be left as a matter for the parents? What if the obesity was starting to impact severely on the life of the child? Or what of parents who believe their religion teaches that corporal punishment should be used to discipline their children, or who require their children to spend hours a day in religious devotion? These are difficult questions.

Here are some models that might be taken in respect of child protection:

- *Parents' rights-focused approach.* Here the law would recognize and support the fact that parents have the right to raise their children as they wish. It might be emphasized that there is little agreement on the best way to bring up children. Perhaps the one thing we might all agree on is that politicians do not know better than anyone else. This approach would advocate a policy which starts with saying that officials should keep out unless the harm to the child is very severe, in which case the child should be removed.

- *Protection.* This approach would emphasize that governments have a special obligation to ensure that the vulnerable in society are well cared for. While we might generally assume that children are well cared for by their parents, where that is not happening the state should step in to offer support to ensure that the children are well looked after, or remove children who cannot be offered a decent standard of care.

- *Children's rights.* Some have argued that the matter must be seen from the child's perspective. We should listen to children who have been abused and seek to fashion a response that meets their wishes and needs. In some cases that might mean assisting parents to be better parents; in other cases staying out; and in others removal of a child from their home. The aim, however, of the law should be to give the child who is suffering harm a voice and power to determine their future.

One point that should become clear as those views are considered is that governments' responses to child abuse need not be limited to an 'all or nothing' approach. In many cases the response will be to support the parents to do a better job. Most social workers would rather provide support and help to the parents than remove a child. Indeed health visitors/visiting nurses, social workers, teachers, and doctors are all involved in encouraging parents to behave in a particular way. This 'soft' policing of family is designed to avoid more formal interventions to protect children.

Human rights

Courts sometimes see child protection issues in human rights terms. At one level there is the inevitable clash between the right to private and family life of the family unit and the right of the child to protection from violence. Lady Hale, an English judge, put the dilemma well:

> In a free society, it is a serious thing indeed for the state compulsorily to remove a child from his family of birth. Interference with the right to respect for family life, protected by article 8 of the European Convention on Human Rights, can only be justified by a pressing social need. Yet it is also a serious thing for the state to fail to safeguard its children from the neglect and ill-treatment which they may suffer in their own homes. This may even amount to a violation of their right not to be subjected to inhuman or degrading treatment, protected by article 3 of the Convention. How then is the law to protect the family from unwarranted intrusion while at the same time protecting children from harm?

The presentation of a 'clash' between these two rights might be misconceived. Where the family life is one characterized by abuse of a child, the courts might appropriately decide that it is not family life which is deserving of 'respect for family life'. So it is not so much protection of the child trumping the right to family life, there is no family life that deserves protection.

This argument, however, is not as convincing when the abuse is at a lesser level. Then, for many commentators, the notion of proportionality becomes key. This is the principle that the extent of state intervention in family life should be proportionate to the harm threatened to the child. Putting it more strongly, the extent of the intervention should be the least necessary to ensure the protection of the child. If the court can find a less intrusive way of protecting the child than that which is proposed, it should reject the proposal.

Criminal law

The law's primary response to the abuse of children is the criminal law. Children, like anyone else, can be the victims of the normal array of crimes. Most legal systems also have a series of offences designed to protect children from mistreatment and sexual abuse. For example, in America there is the Child Abuse Prevention and Treatment Act of 1974. More controversially some countries have offences which punish those who fail to protect children from the abuse of others. These are controversial because sometimes mothers are prosecuted for failing to protect children from a violent father, even though he is abusing the mother as well as the child.

Outside the criminal law, the law places a range of obligations on local authorities to provide services and accommodation to children in need. English legislation puts positive obligations on local authorities to protect children. Indeed these have been said by the European Court of Human Rights to be required under human rights laws. These are primarily designed to prevent a family reaching the position where the child is suffering significant harm. Similarly, the court can make a family assistance order which authorizes the local authority to ascertain the needs of a family and provide services. However, most attention focuses on the more extreme cases where the local authority seeks the removal of a child.

Under English law three things must be shown before a care order can be made and a child removed from her or his parents:

1. The court must be satisfied that 'the child concerned is suffering, or is likely to suffer, significant harm'.

2. '[T]hat the harm, or likelihood of harm, is attributable to: (i) the care given to the child, or likely to be given to him if the order were not made, not being what it would be reasonable to expect a parent to give him; or (ii) the child's being beyond parental control.'

3. The making of the order would promote the welfare of the child.

Other jurisdictions have in place a similar set of conditions which must be met before a child can be removed from the parent. There are a number of things which are notable about these criteria. First, the harm must be significant. Here the law is ensuring that only in the most serious cases can the child be removed from the parents. Second, the criteria include not just that the child has suffered significant harm, but also that the child may be likely to suffer significant harm. This is interesting because it opens the possibility of a child being removed from parents who have not yet harmed a child, but where it is likely that they will. Third, it must be shown that the harm is attributable to the care the child has received (or that the child is out of parental control). This protects parents whose child is suffering through no fault of their own. It might be the child is disabled, or living in a deprived environment, for example. This is not quite as narrow a requirement as might appear. If a child is being abused by an uncle, it may be seen that the harm is attributable to the parents, if they could have protected the child from the abuse.

There are still, of course, many tricky issues to decide. To what extent should the cultural or religious background of a family be considered in determining whether there is child abuse? How should a court deal with a case where it is unclear whether the abuse was carried out by the mother or the father? What about a case where there are lots of suspicious circumstances, but there is no proof as to what has happened? There are no hard and fast answers to these questions. Generally the courts take a flexible approach so that they can resolve the issue based on the facts of the case.

The result of care proceedings

It is falsely imagined that if a care order is made the child will be permanently removed from their parents. While that will happen in more serious cases, it is not automatic. A child may be left with the parent, but under close supervision, with the warning that the child can be removed without notice if there are any concerns. Alternatively the child may be removed so that the parents have the chance to receive assistance and education, to enable them to have the child returned. That might be the appropriate response where the root of the concerns is the parents' alcohol misuse, for example. Where it is thought appropriate for a child to be taken into care permanently, adoption is a popular alternative.

Adoption

The history of adoption is fascinating. Traditionally adoption was seen as a convenient way of handing children born to an unmarried mother to a married, infertile couple. It was seen as a blessing to all concerned: the unmarried mother could quietly and without embarrassment get rid of the child, who would otherwise be a public witness to her sin, and the married couple would be provided with the child they so longed for. Nowadays, given the availability of abortion and the loss of stigma on unmarried parenthood, few are likely to feel compelled to give a child up for adoption. Infertile couples may turn to assisted reproductive technology, rather than adoption. The use of adoption today is very different. It is seen as the best way to provide long-term care for children who have been taken into care or whose parents are unable to look after their needs.

Traditionally adoption has relied on the 'transplant' model, and it still does in America and Britain. Under this approach when an adoption order is made a child ceases to be a member of the 'old family' and becomes a child of the 'new family'. This means that adoptive parents and children have all the legal rights that other parents and children have. The birth parents lose their status entirely. This model suited the old-fashioned use of adoption. The birth parents did not want to retain any link with the embarrassment of having the baby out of wedlock, and the infertile couple would want to be regarded as full parents. However the transplant model works less well with the current use of adoption.

This is why. Most children who are adopted are now older and will have memories of their birth parents. So any idea that we can trick children into believing their adoptive parents are their biological parents will be a fiction. Further, the children are likely to wish to retain some links with their birth family, if not their parents then their grandparents or aunts and uncles. That may make a model based on a complete break from the birth family inappropriate. Finally, many children who are available for adoption have suffered traumatic experiences or have disabilities or difficulties. The adoptive parents may well need extensive support and advice from the local authority, unlike the infertile couple adopters of the past who would be given healthy babies and not need particular help.

Despite these points, adoption has become well established in Western societies. It offers a high level of security for those couples preparing to undertake a major commitment to a child. If people are going to throw themselves into taking on the care of a child they are likely to require the kind of legal protections that are given to parents.

'Special guardianship' was introduced in the UK in 2006 partly as a result of the concerns over the transplant model. This grants someone who is to be a long-term carer of a child the rights and responsibilities of being a parent, without making them the parent in the eyes of the law. This is designed particularly in cases where a relative is taking on the care of a child and it might seem inappropriate for, say, the child's grandparent to become their parent.

Who can adopt?

In the US, regulations on who can adopt vary from state to state, ranging from only allowing married couples to adopt, to having few restrictions. England has surprisingly liberal laws on who can adopt. Since the 2002 Adoption and Children Act an adopter can be a couple, be they married or unmarried, be they same-sex or opposite sex, or indeed a single person. The adopters must, however, be 21 or over. The width of these categories was justified on the basis that the focus should be on the best interests of the particular child. If the applicants were the most suitable people for adopters then they should be able to adopt, regardless of their marital status or sexual orientation.

The regulation of adoption

There is a striking difference between adoption in England and the US. In England private adoptions are not permitted. Adoption can only take place through an approved adoption agency. These agencies are required to select from the range of approved adopters. Someone wanting to adopt a child must be approved by an adoption agency, which will undertake a lengthy and in-depth consideration of their suitability. Many would-be adopters will not make it through to this stage. Even if they do, there tend to be more parents seeking adoption than children available. No money will change hands.

Conclusion

Everyone agrees that child abuse is a terrible thing and society must prevent it. But this consensus breaks down when it comes to legal intervention. What should be done when there is suspicion but no proven abuse? How bad must the abuse be before it justifies removal of the child? These are difficult questions on which reasonable people can disagree, but judges have to determine day in, day out.

Chapter 7
Alimony and financial orders

On legal separation couples seek court orders to resolve disputes over finances. These can produce ferocious arguments. In one case a man divorcing his wife sought the return of his kidney that he donated to her when she needed a transplant! That may be extreme, but there is a widespread perception that divorce causes financial ruin for the wealthy. In truth, divorce often causes financial ruin, particularly for women.

Child support

Perhaps the least controversial principle on financial order is that a parent should support their child. Sadly this principle is honoured as much in the breach as the observance. Twenty-seven per cent of all children in the UK live in poverty. In part, that is due to a failure of parents, typically those absent from children, in providing adequate support. But in blaming child poverty on parents not paying financial support we are making some assumptions. Why should parents be liable to support children? Further how should we balance the obligations of the state and parents towards the cost of raising a child? Is the duty of the state to ensure provision for children and to provide the shortfall where it fails or is the state's responsibility limited to providing a means for enforcing the provision? The best answer may lie between these two extremes. American Law Professor Harry Krause suggests that the obligation is shared between society and the parents: 'children have a right to a decent start in life. This right is the obligation of the father and equally of the mother, and in recognition of a primary and direct responsibility, equally the obligation of society.'

The debate over child support has involved issues around what many people call the 'crisis of lone parents'. In 2011 in England and Wales 26 per cent of households with a child were headed by a lone parent. The same percentage is recorded for the US in 2009. In 1971, the figure was 8 per cent. To some this is a crisis with children in lone-parent households facing poverty and lower levels of parenting. Of course it might be more accurate to refer to the problem of non-resident fathers than lone mothers. It is the failure of fathers. Lady Thatcher, who as Prime Minister had steered the Child Support Act 1991 through Parliament, notably recalled in her memoirs that she was 'appalled by the way in which men fathered a child and then absconded, leaving the single mother—and the tax payer—to foot the bill for their irresponsibility and condemning the child to a lower standard of living'.

I would suggest the starting point in discussing financial orders is children's rights. Children should have a right to enough financial support to ensure they are fed, clothed, and given the essential provisions to thrive. These the state must provide, but the form of that provision can vary:

- The state could provide benefits and/or tax breaks to parents to assist in the financial cost of raising children. Of course, this would carry dangers. It cannot be assumed that any extra cash given to parents will, in fact, be spent on children. There may be ways of limiting the danger of this if the assistance is provided in terms of food vouchers, but these can be seen as stigmatizing and offer little guarantee that the food purchased will be consumed by children.

- An alternative is simply to encourage parents to work. This could be done by providing particular benefits to parents seeking work or assistance with childcare or other expenses that might otherwise be a disincentive to work. This policy may combat child poverty, especially in lone-parent households, but may do nothing in cases where the parent cannot, for whatever reason, undertake employment. Indeed if such an approach was the sole form of support for children, those parents with a severely disabled child might be particularly hard hit.

- A third option would be for the state to encourage the non-resident parent to pay support. In England the Child Support Agency, a government body, was created to collect payments from non-resident parents.

For a family lawyer, it is this third option which is of greatest interest. It raises a number of complex issues. First, is the obligation to support a child shared between the parents so that each can be required to pay half or can each be liable individually for the total amount needed? Is a non-resident father only required to pay half the amount of money needed to support the child, on the basis that he is only half of the parental team? Further, if the resident parent is very wealthy and easily able to pay expenses is the non-resident parent liable to pay? Against both these arguments may be a claim that the resident parent has to undertake the day-to-day care and so it is fair that the non-resident parent must pay their portion of child support.

Second, there is the question of who counts as a parent for these purposes. Imagine A (a man) and B (a woman) have a child, Y. A moves out and later lives with C, who has a child, X, by a previous relationship. Should A support Y or X? Or should he try to support both? It is not difficult to imagine a man supporting a child living in another household, while another man supports the child living with him. Some say in cases like that it makes more sense to expect the man to support the child living with him. Indeed, you could imagine a case where a father's current partner and child are in poverty while he pays child support to his well-off ex-wife and child.

A rather different issue is that of the so-called 'sperm bandits'. Some men have claimed that while asleep or drunk women have extracted their sperm and thereby rendered them biological fathers. Others have argued they were deceived by women into believing the women were using birth control. Should such 'unintentional fathers' be burdened with child support obligations? Some would make the point in relation to all casual sexual encounters. As American lawyer Marshall Kapp has argued:

> To saddle a man with at least eighteen years of expensive, exhausting child support liability on the basis of a haphazard vicissitude of life seems to shock the conscience and be arbitrary, capricious, and unreasonable, where childbirth results from the mother's free choice...a man no longer has any control over the course of a pregnancy he has biologically brought about [and] it is unjust to impose responsibility where there is no ability to exercise control.

While many will feel that expecting child support would be unfair on men in some cases, one response is that this is justified from the perspective of the rights of children.

Even if these issues are covered what should be the level of financial support offered? Should it be set at what a child needs for subsistence? Or at an acceptable standard of living? Should the level be at what the child might have been expected to enjoy had the parents not separated? If a millionaire fathers a child should she be expected therefore to have the life of a millionaire's child?

Spousal support

Although the idea that on divorce the court can redistribute the assets of a couple and order payments of alimony or maintenances is now largely taken for granted, the court is in fact exercising the most extraordinary power. Every penny that a person has can be taken from them and given to someone else. Not only that, but they can be required to hand over every penny that they earn in the future. Of course it is unlikely that a court would make such an extreme order. But the power to do so is remarkable.

Divorce marks financial ruin for many people. The assets and income that barely supported the family household must now support two households. Divorce nearly always means significant downsizing. But the impact of divorce is often gendered. While women may initially seem to do better on divorce, the long-term impact is largely negative. The conclusions of a recent UK study on the impact of divorce on women was blunt:

> The stark conclusion is that men's household income increases by about 23 per cent on divorce once we control for household size, whereas women's household income falls by about 31 per cent. There is partial recovery for women, but this recovery is driven by repartnering: the average effect of repartnering is to restore income to pre-divorce levels after nine years. [For] those who do not repartner...the long term economic consequences of divorce are serious.

Why is divorce so bad for women? The answer lies in what happens during marriage. During the marriage, even nowadays, women undertake the bulk of childcare and housework. Their employment opportunities are thereby reduced. When couples make decisions about work most often decisions are made in relation to what will improve the husband's opportunity, not the wife's. Marriage therefore typically causes a serious setback to the woman's employment opportunities and an improvement to those of the man. This occurs not only during the marriage, but has long-term implications. Childcare obligations may continue in the future causing further financial disadvantage. Court orders on divorce, then, are seeking to ensure there is a fair share of the financial benefits and disadvantages of the marriage.

However the issue is not straightforward and there are plenty of other issues at play here. One is that many couples may, understandably, wish to have independent lives after divorce. We do not want spouses to feel yoked together forever. They should not be dependent on the other for financial support for any longer than necessary. Sometimes this leads the court to make a 'clean break' order, whereby the richer spouse (typically the husband) hands over most of the assets to his wife, and in return she agrees there will be no ongoing liability. This is seen by some couples as preferable to a more equal sharing of the assets, with ongoing maintenance. Preferable to the wife because she is free from concerns that the husband might reduce or stop payments if she repartners or finds a job. Preferable to the husband because he need not be concerned that the wife will seek an increase in payments if his income increases. Despite the attractions of this kind of solution, most couples do not have enough assets to provide the wife with a sufficient capital sum to make up for not having ongoing payments.

Theories of spousal redistribution

There are a multitude of theories for why one spouse should support another following separation. I will highlight the main ones. Of course, there is no need to adopt only one of these. They can operate in tandem, although used separately the sums of money produced may be quite different.

Spousal support and the care of children

A degree of spousal support can be justified simply in terms of child support. Once it is accepted a parent must support a child, that must include support for someone who is looking after the child. You can deliver all the nappies/diapers, food, and soap to the child you like, but there has to be someone to clothe, feed, and clean the child.

Breach of contract

A second approach is to regard a divorce as a breach of contract, for which the spouse must pay damages. As marriage is a promise to stay together until death then the richer spouse should pay the poorer enough money to live the kind of lifestyle they would have enjoyed until death. This approach is certainly problematic. Some would see it as based on an outdated model. Do we really take it nowadays that marriage involves a promise to stay together until death? Even if we do, the law does not generally attempt to find out who has breached the contract and whether there was contributory negligence.

Partnership

Probably the view with the most popularity is that marriage should be seen as analogous to a partnership. The spouses cooperate together as part of a joint economic enterprise. As often happens in a business they carry out different roles within the enterprise, but there should be a fair sharing of the benefits and burdens of the relationship. Lord Nicholls in the leading decision of *Miller v Miller* in England, put it this way:

> [in marriage] the parties commit themselves to sharing their lives. They live and work together. When their partnership ends each is entitled to an equal share of the assets of the partnership, unless there is a good reason to the contrary. Fairness requires no less.

This might represent a rather outdated view of marriage, when marriage marked the start of cohabitation and joint lives. Nowadays people have typically lived together for quite some time before marriage. Marriage is rarely the start of an intertwining of lives, but the expression of a complete interconnection. It could also be argued that on marriage the parties will bring to the relationship a variety of different assets, skills, personalities, interests, etc. Throughout the marriage each party will enjoy and share their personalities, interests, and skills. If the relationship involves the mutual sharing of all aspects of their lives, this should include their material assets.

Even if one is attracted to the partnership model there are difficulties with its application. First, there is the question of what is included within the definition of marital assets, generated during the partnership. Is it to include the earning capacity that a spouse has developed, for example? Second, does the law have to assume that the parties' contribution to the enterprise is equal? Is a contribution by means of childcare equal to a financial contribution, regardless of whether the income is tiny or massive?

Compensation

Another justification for financial orders rests on compensation. The partnership theory argues that couples should share in the benefits generated by the relationship. The compensation model argues that couples should share in the disadvantages. If during the relationship one partner has suffered loss by giving up a well-paid job to undertake childcare or other family work for the good of the couple, they should be compensated for losses caused. This compensation could include the loss of earning potential.

A rather different form of the argument is that the non-earning spouse should, in retrospect, be paid an appropriate wage for her or his work by the other spouse. A court could assess how much the house-cleaning and child-caring would have cost had people been employed to do it. Some who adopt this approach accept that, as the non-earning spouse benefits from the housework, the cost should be shared and so the earning spouse should only pay for half of this work.

Not everyone is convinced by these compensation arguments. It might be argued that if a woman had not married her husband she would have married someone else, and so it is not realistic to claim that the lack of development in her career is this one man's fault; although such arguments overlook the benefits provided to the particular husband through the care she undertook.

The state interest in childcare

Underpinning many of these issues is the attitude of the state towards childcare. The state might take the view that each member of society should be as economically productive as possible, and so it would want to discourage a spouse giving up employment to take up childcare, in which case the state might want to limit financial awards on divorce. If there were no financial orders on divorce then this would discourage a spouse from thinking of giving up employment to care for children; instead they would be likely to rely on day care. However, the state might believe that children's interests are promoted if one spouse gives up work to care for the children, in which case some form of protection from financial disadvantage would be necessary.

Indeed some feminists have called for the abolition of maintenance payments for women, arguing that the existence of maintenance perpetuates the fact that women are dependent upon men. A vicious circle exists in that, because the law tells wives that they will be entitled to financial support if their relationship ends, they are willing to take lower-paid jobs and they thereby do become dependent upon their husbands. If maintenance were abolished and financial independence encouraged, women would have to find jobs that paid adequately. This is, however, a minority view among feminists. Most argue that women should be able to choose whether to work or care and both should be valued.

Orders the court can make

The following are the kind of orders a court can make on divorce:

- Income orders: these typically require monthly payments from one spouse to the other. Typically they are limited either in time (e.g. for three years) or in relation to an event (e.g. they will cease on remarriage).

- Lump sum orders. These are orders that one spouse pay the other a fixed sum of money.

- Property orders. These can require that property that is jointly owned (e.g. a house) be transferred to one spouse or be sold and the proceeds divided.

- Pension order. Some jurisdictions have orders where one spouse can be required to give up a share of their pension to the other.

The law on property orders on divorce is partly influenced by the law on ownership of property during marriage. There are three primary regimes. Under the common law system marriage does not affect ownership of property and each spouse owns what they acquire during the marriage. Under a community of property regime the couple shares property that either of them acquires during the marriage. The third regime is less common nowadays and holds that on marriage the couple equally share all property that they own, be that property acquired before or during the marriage.

It is rare for couples who are married to dispute ownership so these rules come to the fore on divorce because they form the backdrop against which a court will make any financial orders. Under a community of property approach, popular particularly in the south-western states of the US, there is less need for significant court orders where the spouses will already be sharing the assets generated during the marriage. With a common law approach if one spouse has been earning income and the other not the ownership of property might be markedly unequal. Under a common law system, when a court is deciding what order to make, the current ownership of property is unlikely to carry much weight.

Disclosure

What actually takes up most of the time in difficult divorce cases is not disputing the appropriate order, but discovering the assets the other party has. One of the first stages in a dispute will be for the lawyers on each side to seek to ascertain the wealth of each party. Typically, a questionnaire will be sent requiring each party to list all of their assets. Experienced lawyers will know to take the responses to these questionnaires with a pinch of salt. Precise questions and investigations, some barely legal, are then used to uncover the truth.

There are procedures available to deal with the more obvious attempts at evading disclosure. If assets have been transferred to third parties for the purposes of escaping payments the court can order these to be returned. Similarly there is scope for orders to disclose particular pieces of information. However, both of these involve expensive applications and unless there is a lot of money involved are unlikely to be worth it. All too often courts have to proceed with only a rough idea of what assets each couple own.

The orders

The precise orders which the court may make will depend on the particular jurisdiction. There follow some general principles which often guide courts in this area.

Needs

In many cases, as already mentioned, divorce brings huge financial hardship for all concerned. Family lawyers will be familiar with the crushed look of a middle-class client realizing that post-divorce they are likely to be living in a rented bedsit or that the days of private schools or exotic holidays are long over. The court will do all it can to ensure the basic needs of parties are met, but sometimes even that is not possible. But it is normally the starting point. How can the assets be used to meet the basic needs of the parties, particularly the children?

Of course, 'needs' is a somewhat flexible concept. The courts tend to interpret it in the context of the kind of lifestyle the couple has enjoyed during their marriage. English courts have sometimes preferred the word 'reasonable requirements' to cover the embarrassment of explaining that a spouse needs substantial sums for clothes or holidays. Typically those seeking a financial order will be required to provide a budget setting out their future needs. Predictably this leads to claims that the other is seeking to live an extravagant lifestyle at their expense.

Equality

This principle is that the couple should share their assets equally. This is typically based on the partnership theory, discussed in the preceding section. As mentioned there, it can take two forms. It can require a sharing of all of the 'marital assets' (the assets generated during the marriage) or it can require a sharing of all the assets the couple have, regardless of when they were generated. It may be that the length of the marriage is a relevant factor here. The longer the marriage, the less pertinent it might be whether an asset was created before or after a marriage.

Compensation

Another principle which has been used by the courts is the argument that the court should ensure that financial compensation is granted to a party who has lost out financially as a result of the marriage. We have already considered this argument.

Conduct

Many people going through a divorce expect, indeed want, the court to place weight on the other party's misconduct. However, the days when a husband who had an affair would have to pay for it on divorce are long gone. The courts are not going to be interested in the bad behaviour of a spouse, save, perhaps, where there have been financial consequences, e.g. where a party had gambled away significant wealth. Generally, only in the most extreme cases will conduct be relevant (see Box 15 and Figure 7).

7. **Paul McCartney and Heather Mills**

Pre-nuptial contracts

Some couples, in preparation for marriage, will sign a pre-nuptial, or pre-marriage contract, which sets out what will happen to their property in the event of a divorce. Typically a wealthier spouse will seek to limit the financial damage of a divorce. This is especially true in cases where there are family assets they wish to ensure will be left to their children.

Box 15 *McCartney v Mills-McCartney* (2008) 1 FCR 707

The husband, Paul McCartney, a famous musician and composer, had been married to Heather Mills for four years. At the time of divorce the wife claimed that the husband was worth £400 million. Justice Bennett held that it was important to note that the vast bulk of the husband's fortune was made before the marriage and indeed before the couple met. The amount of money generated during the marriage was very small. There was no evidence that Heather Mills had suffered a financial loss as a result of the marriage. In the light of these facts the primary focus of the courts would be to ensure that the wife and child's reasonable needs (interpreted in a generous way) were met. Focusing on those, he was ordered to pay her £16.5 million, meaning she would leave the marriage worth £24.3 million. Maintenance for the child was set at £35,000 per annum and the nanny's salary at £30,000.

Jurisdictions have responded differently to these 'pre-nups' (short for pre-nuptial agreements) as they are traditionally known. American law has long been willing to give effect to these agreements. If the parties have decided what financial arrangements would be fair, why should the courts interfere? Most European countries have taken a similar approach, with pre-nups being a routine part of marriage.

English courts have taken a rather different approach. To them it is the role of the courts to determine what orders are fair on divorce. The couple, in entering a pre-nup, is depriving the courts of their Parliament-given role. At one time the argument was also used that it was contrary to public policy for a couple to think about divorce when they were planning to marry. However, in 2010 the UK Supreme Court declared a change in approach so that pre-nups are given effect, so long as it would be fair to do so.

In the UK, it would be wrong to think that where there is a pre-nuptial agreement it will automatically determine the financial order that will be made on divorce. There are two kinds of limitation which a court will impose.

First, the court will need to be convinced that the parties entered into the agreement freely and sufficiently informed. In particular, the courts are likely to consider whether one spouse put undue pressure on the other; whether the parties understood the agreement and received independent advice; and whether there was appropriate disclosure of each party's financial position. These are not requirements as such and a court may be persuaded that an agreement was fairly entered into even though there was not, for example, independent advice, so long as each party understood what they were signing.

Second, the court will not give effect to the agreement where there is manifest unfairness. The extent to which a court might do this will vary according to jurisdiction. Here there is a balance to be struck between protecting the parties and respecting their autonomy. It is highly unlikely that an agreement will be given effect to if it fails to provide adequately for the children. Similarly, if events occur during the marriage which were utterly unforeseen and lead to a harsh impact on one of the spouses a court may be persuaded to depart from the agreement.

Commentators have divided on the benefits of pre-nups. To some they provide the parties with the means of deciding for themselves what is fair and reasonable, rather than have a judge tell them what is fair. For others pre-nups require the parties to do the impossible in imagining what would be fair in the event of a divorce, possibly years down the line. The best-laid plans may need to be set aside on the birth of a severely disabled child, or the illness of a parent, or unexpected unemployment. Perhaps the strongest argument against pre-nups is that they fail to acknowledge the public significance of the orders made on divorce. As Baroness Hale, an English Supreme Court Justice, put it:

> Would any self-respecting young woman sign up to an agreement which assumed that she would be the only one who might otherwise have a claim, thus placing no limit on the claims that might be made against her, and then limit her claim to a pre-determined sum for each year of marriage regardless of the circumstances, as if her wifely services were being bought by the year? Yet that is what these precedents do.

At the heart of the debate over pre-nups is the nature of marriage. It is the question of whether marriage is a status or a contract, discussed in Chapter 1. Most countries take a hybrid approach. You can control the terms of your marriage contract to some extent, but if the courts regard what has been agreed as too unfair then they will override it.

This explains why many jurisdictions are more relaxed about cohabitation contracts. As unmarried couples are not in a formal relationship they are, in a legal sense, strangers and free to contract with each other, just like anyone else. The married couples have chosen to join the 'club' of being married and cannot unilaterally determine the rules of the club. The growth of pre-nups, and increased legal recognition of them, means we are witnessing a shift towards a more individualized understanding of marriage. It is less like a club and more like a number of private dinner parties.

Unmarried couples and divorce

When an unmarried couple separates the courts do not have the extensive powers that they have on divorce in most countries.

Normally the courts are limited to simply declaring who owns what property, using the normal law on property. There is no power to require one party to give the other party money. Of course, if there are children child support must be paid, but that does not include financial support specifically for the other parent. Some unmarried couples will enter cohabitation contracts to ensure there is some financial protection in the event of a breakdown of the relationship.

That said, some courts have been quite creative in developing property law rules so that in the case of a lengthy cohabitation it is very likely a property will be found to be jointly owned (see the American case of *Marvin v Marvin*, discussed in Chapter 1). Other jurisdictions, such New Zealand and Australia, have developed special rules to apply to cohabiting couples so that after two years of cohabitation the court has the power to redistribute property, unless the couple have opted out of the regime.

Conclusion

The problem of finding a suitable way of dividing assets on divorce reflects broader problems in society. It is because our society does not adequately recognize the value of childcare, or of the care of dependent relatives, that marriage can cause economic hardship. It is because in many marriages care work is not spread equally between couples that the economic benefits and disadvantages are not shared equally. In short, financial orders are seeking to remedy the problems generated by broader social failures.

Chapter 8
Where next for family law?

As may be clear from this book family law is undergoing huge changes because family life is undergoing huge changes. The traditional building blocks of family law—marriage, parenthood, home, childhood—are being changed before our eyes at a bewildering pace. The law is, frankly, struggling to keep up. In this chapter I identify three of the key battlegrounds which I expect will emerge as the law seeks to find an appropriate response to the realities of family life in the twenty-first century.

Individual versus relational values

Should family law focus on the protection of individual rights and interests; or should it seek to promote relationships? Are the values that we would wish to promote those of autonomy, freedom, and self-determination; or responsibilities to each other and a recognition of mutual obligations? I expect for many people the answer to both these questions is that we want to value all of these things. The question is, how can we go about doing that? How can we recognize the responsibilities of family life in a way which does not impact on individual freedom? Yet not recognizing the responsibilities of family life will mean that people will not be able to enter intimate, caring relationships without fear of being left with an unfair share of the burdens.

We can see some of the tensions here in issues like financial orders on divorce. Do we expect partners to be financially independent and responsible for their own economic well-being or do we want the law to ensure the benefits and disadvantages of the relationship are shared equally?

The difficulty is that the law typically promotes the values of privacy, autonomy, and independence. In short the law works well at keeping other people out. Yet family law is all about relationships and keeping together. In families notions of privacy and individual autonomy do not fit into the way families work. Families do not typically see themselves as individuals with rights that clash with each other, but as a group of people seeking to work together for their common good.

Gender and family life

The consequences of family life and the impact of family law are hugely relevant to our assumptions relating to gender. Historically women have had a bad deal in families. Their care work has been unrecognized; their status as mother downgraded; and violence against them left unpunished and even justified. Family Law, through its understandings of a 'good mother' and its response to care work, can impact, or at least reflect, broader social responses to women in family life.

It is interesting that in recent times the loudest voices in the media often claim that the pendulum has now swung against men. It is said that the courts fail to acknowledge the importance of men in children's lives and too often men are denied contact with their children on divorce. Further, complaints are made that child support and spousal support payments are so high that they are manifestly unfair to men.

As societal attitudes towards the roles expected of mothers and fathers and spouses change, in part through the reimagining of family life in same-sex relationships, it will be interesting to see how family law develops. One thing is for sure, it is unlikely that debates over whether family law is unfair to men or unfair to women will die away.

Society and family law

It is commonly said that family life is a private matter and that the state should not seek to intrude into people's intimate lives. There is, of course, much truth in that. Family life which was subject to constant state surveillance would be miserable. If governments were to try to force all families to be the same this would rob society of the diversity which gives it its colour and fun. Certainly the days when judges would make rulings based on whether they thought one family member had behaved in a moral or immoral way tend to be long gone.

There is, however, a growing recognition that what happens in family life is important for society. The way our children are cared for, the problems of domestic abuse, the gender inequalities in household work, and the care of the elderly are all issues of huge social significance. However, none of these issues is easy to address. The correct response to these requires a careful balance of legal intervention, education, and a change in societal expectations and behaviour.

The future?

I don't believe for a moment the future will see the end of family life. Intimate relationships, the creation and raising of children, the care of the elderly will not go away. In the past these were done, typically, within the formal structure of marriage. Nowadays there is a broader range of relationships within which these things happen. Some have written of the growth of individualism, with people seeking personal gratification and throwing off the ties of family responsibility. There are a few who do that. But the vast majority of parents still feel a strong obligation towards their children. Most people still feel a strong obligation to ensure suitable care for their elderly parents. What I suggest we are seeing is a shift in the basis of familial responsibilities. A shift away from the obligations that flow from duties based on status—what a person ought to do as a spouse or a parent—towards duties based on the actual relationship between the parties. A person who has a close relationship to a child will feel obligated to that child, whether there is a blood tie or not. It may be that in the future, rather than marriage and parenthood, friendship and care will become the building blocks of family law.

Further reading

This book does not, of course, purport to provide legal advice for a particular problem you may be facing. For that you must consult a specialist family lawyer. Here are some further readings on the issues addressed in this book

Overviews of family law

S. Gilmore, *Family Law* (Oxford: Oxford University Press, 2012).

J. Herring, *Family Law* (5th edn.) (Harlow: Pearson, 2011).

S. Katz, *Family Law in America* (New York: Oxford University Press, 2011).

American family law differs hugely from state to state but Katz's book provides a wonderful overview of the topic. My textbook on family law and that by Gilmore provide a detailed discussion of English family law and wider theoretical debates over family life.

Chapter 1: Marriage, civil partnership, and cohabitation

E. Brake, *Minimizing Marriage* (Oxford: Oxford University Press, 2012).

J. Eekelaar, *Family Life and Personal Life* (Oxford: Oxford University Press, 2006).

M. Fineman, *The Autonomy Myth* (New York: The New Press, 2004).

M. Lyndon Shanley, *Just Marriage* (Oxford: Oxford University Press, 2004).

R. Probert, *The Changing Legal Regulation of Cohabitation* (Cambridge: Cambridge University Press, 2012).

M. Regan, *Alone Together: Law and the Meaning of Marriage* (Oxford: Oxford University Press, 1999).

These books explore in different ways changes in the nature of marriage and how we regulate family life. Fineman's book provides a powerful critique of the way that marriage has privatized care work and thereby worked against the interests of children. That can be contrasted with Regan's book which is more positive about the role of marriage. Brake, Eekelaar, and Lyndon Shanley explore ways in which marriage and family law could be reimagined in the future. Probert's book focuses on those who do not marry and the difficulties the law has faced in regulating their relationships.

Chapter 2: Domestic violence

M. Madden Dempsey, *Prosecuting Domestic Violence* (Oxford: Oxford University Press, 2009).

E. Schneider, *Battered Women and Feminist Law Making* (New Haven: Yale University Press, 2000).

E. Stark, *Coercive Control: How Men Entrap Women in Personal Life* (Oxford: Oxford University Press, 2007).

These books explore the legal response to domestic violence. Madden Dempsey focuses on the criminal law response, while Stark focuses on the nature of domestic violence. Schneider brings to light the failure of the law to respond adequately to domestic violence.

Chapter 3: Divorce

J. Eekelaar, *Regulating Divorce* (Oxford: Clarendon Press, 1991).
H. Reece, *Divorcing Responsibly* (Oxford: Hart, 2003).

These two books provide powerful discussion of the law on divorce, looking at what the law is seeking to do and the extent to which the law can, or cannot, influence the behaviour of divorcing couples.

Chapter 4: Parents

A. Bainham, S. Day Sclater, and M. Richards (eds.), *What is a Parent?* (Oxford: Hart, 1999).

J. Bridgeman, *Parental Responsibility, Young Children and Healthcare Law* (Cambridge: Cambridge University Press, 2007).

R. Collier and S. Sheldon, *Fragmenting Fatherhood* (Oxford: Hart, 2008).

K. Horsey and H. Biggs, *Human Fertilisation and Embryology: Reproducing Regulation* (London: Routledge, 2007).

The Bainham, Day Sclater, and Richards edited book provides an excellent set of essays from lawyers, philosophers, and sociologists on the nature of parenthood. Collier and Sheldon give a fascinating look at the nature of fatherhood in modern society. In her book Bridgeman presents a sensitive examination of how the law should regulate parental decisions. Horsey and Biggs explore how the law's understanding of parenthood has been challenged by technological advances.

Chapter 5: Children's rights

D. Archard, *Children: Rights and Childhood* (London: Routledge, 2006).

J. Fortin, *Children's Rights and the Developing Law* (London: LexisNexis Butterworths, 2009).

M. Guggenheim, *What's Wrong with Children's Rights?* (Cambridge, Mass.: Harvard University Press, 2005).

M. King and C. Piper, *How the Law Thinks about Children* (Aldershot: Arena, 1995).

These books provide insightful analysis of the issues around child abuse. Guggenheim stands out as a book which is more sceptical of the benefit of children's rights. The King and Piper book issues a stark warning about how concepts of children's welfare can become distorted in legal analysis.

Chapter 6: Child abuse

D. Archard, *The Family: A Liberal Defence* (Houndmills: Palgrave, 2010).

L. Fox Harding, *Family, State and Social Policy* (Houndmills: Macmillan, 1996).

L. Hoyano and C. Keenan, *Child Abuse: Law and Policy across Boundaries* (Oxford: Oxford University Press, 2007).

Further reading

Hoyano and Keenan provide a sensitive, but powerful, analysis of the issues around child abuse. Archard considers the arguments for why we assume families are a safe place to bring up children. The Fox Harding book looks at the relationship between the state and families.

Chapter 7: Alimony and financial orders

J. Herring, R. Probert, and S. Gilmore, *Great Debates: Family Law* (Houndmills: Palgrave, 2012).
N. Wikeley, *Child Support: Law and Policy* (Oxford: Hart, 2006).

The Herring, Probert, and Gilmore book has a fascinating discussion of the different theoretical models underpinning financial orders on divorce. Wikeley's book is a masterful analysis of the issues around child support.

Family Law

Index

A

Adoption 88–90
Age discrimination 67–70
Alimony 92–108

B

Broccoli 69

C

Canterbury, Archbishop of 47
Causes of divorce 46
Ceremony 4
Children Act 1989 58–9
Child abuse 79–91
Child Abuse Prevention and
    Treatment Act 1974 86
Child care 99–100
Child liberation 68–9
Children's rights 67–78, 84
Child support 92–5
Child Support Agency 94
Christianity 4, 47
Civil Partnership Act 2004 17
Constitutional right 7,
    41, 76
Consummation 14
Contact 62–5

Contract 8–9
Criminal Law 35–7

D

Divorce 42–51
Divorce statistics 43–4
DNA 52
Domestic abuse 7, 27–41
Dwyer, James 56

E

Eekelaar, John 72
Elizabeth I 5
Equality 103

F

Farsen, Richard 68
Fault-based divorce 48–9
Fineman, Martha 5
Forced marriage 14–15
Freeman, Michael 72
Friendship 2–3

G

Gay marriage 16–20
Gender 110–11

Gender Recognition Act 2004 13
Giddens, Antony 27, 44
Goodman, Alissa 23
Grandparents 60
Greaves, Ellen 23

H

Hale, Lady 85, 107
Holt, John 68
Human rights 40-1, 75-7,
84, 85-6

I

Intersex people 12
Istanbul Convention 41
IVF 54

K

Kapp, Marshall 95
Krause, Harry 92-3

L

Lasch, Christopher 27
Lesbian parents 56
Local Government Act 1988 2
Lone parents 93

M

Madden Dempsey, Michelle 28-9
Marriage 4-20, 22-6
McCartney, Paul 46, 104-5
Mental disorder 15
Mills, Heather 104-5
Molestation 37-8

N

National Marriage Project 23
Naturism 59-60
Nicholls, Lord 98

No fault divorce 49
Non-marriage 10

O

O'Neill, Onora 75

P

Parents 52-6
Parkinson, Patrick 18-19
Pensions 101
Pre-nups 104-07
Presumption of marriage 9
Prizzy, Erin 35

R

Residence 62-3

S

Sachs, Justice Abie 18
Same-sex relationship 2, 16-20
Schneider, Elizabeth 34
Sexless family law 19-20
Status 8-9
Surrogacy 57-8

T

Trans people 12-13

U

UN Convention on the Rights of
the Child 67
Unregulated relationships 20-1
Unmarried couples 2, 107-8

V

Visitation 63-5
Void marriage 10-13
Voidable marriages 10-14

SOCIAL MEDIA
Very Short Introduction

Join our community

www.oup.com/vsi

- Join us online at the official Very Short Introductions **Facebook** page.
- Access the thoughts and musings of our authors with our online **blog**.
- Sign up for our monthly **e-newsletter** to receive information on all new titles publishing that month.
- Browse the full range of Very Short Introductions online.
- Read **extracts** from the Introductions for free.
- Visit our library of **Reading Guides**. These guides, written by our expert authors will help you to question again, why you think what you think.
- If you are a teacher or lecturer you can order inspection copies quickly and simply via our website.

Visit the Very Short Introductions website to access all this and more for free.
www.oup.com/vsi

ONLINE CATALOGUE
A Very Short Introduction

Our online catalogue is designed to make it easy to find your ideal Very Short Introduction. View the entire collection by subject area, watch author videos, read sample chapters, and download reading guides.

http://fds.oup.com/www.oup.co.uk/general/vsi/index.html

HUMAN RIGHTS
A Very Short Introduction
Andrew Clapham

An appeal to human rights in the face of injustice can be a heartfelt and morally justified demand for some, while for others it remains merely an empty slogan. Taking an international perspective and focusing on highly topical issues such as torture, arbitrary detention, privacy, health and discrimination, this *Very Short Introduction* will help readers to understand for themselves the controversies and complexities behind this vitally relevant issue. Looking at the philosophical justification for rights, the historical origins of human rights and how they are formed in law, Andrew Clapham explains what our human rights actually are, what they might be, and where the human rights movement is heading.

www.oup.com/vsi

LAW
A Very Short Introduction
Raymond Wacks

Law underlies our society - it protects our rights, imposes duties on each of us, and establishes a framework for the conduct of almost every social, political, and economic activity. The punishment of crime, compensation of the injured, and the enforcement of contracts are merely some of the tasks of a modern legal system. It also strives to achieve justice, promote freedom, and protect our security. This *Very Short Introduction* provides a clear, jargon-free account of modern legal systems, explaining how the law works both in the Western tradition and around the world.

www.oup.com/vsi